ABRAHAM LINCOLN
A Biographic Trilogy in Sonnet Sequence

Volume Two

ABRAHAM LINCOLN: THE MAN

OTHER BOOKS
By
DELLA CROWDER MILLER

The Awakening .... a play
Counting Your Blessings .... a pageant
And So Through the Year .... poetry
Old Peter Friend's Pet Animals .... stories
and
Other Volumes of this Lincoln Trilogy
Volume I .... Abraham Lincoln: The Boy
Volume III .... Abraham Lincoln: The President

ABRAHAM LINCOLN

*A BIOGRAPHIC TRILOGY
IN SONNET SEQUENCE*

By

DELLA CROWDER MILLER

Edited By
ORVILLE CROWDER MILLER

Volume Two

ABRAHAM LINCOLN: THE MAN

(Annotated and *Illustrated)*

THE CHRISTOPHER PUBLISHING HOUSE
BOSTON, U.S.A.

ABRAHAM LINCOLN

A Biographic Trilogy in Sonnet Sequence

Volume Two

COPYRIGHT © 1965
By
DELLA CROWDER MILLER
(All Rights Reserved)

Library of Congress Catalog Card Number 64-22912

PRINTED IN
THE UNITED STATES OF AMERICA

TO
THE MEMORY OF
MY FOUR GRANDPARENTS
ROBERT AND BARBARA CROWDER
AND
JAMES MADISON AND JEMIMA WEAR
Of
Marrowbone, Illinois

PREFACE TO VOLUME TWO

THE MAKING OF A MAN
1831-1861

Is there a living man who would attain
Abe Lincoln's fame? Then let him know defeat,
Discouragement and doubt, yet dare to meet
Courageously earth's trials and its pain.
He must be honest, with a will to gain
The highest peak; make each man friend, delete
The good from bad, the false from true; complete
His climb by welding links throughout his chain.

Abe Lincoln mastered self, then mastered men:
He felt unjust attacks—their sting and smart—
Then, while his load was heaviest, he spun
Some yarn or joke that let him laugh again;
But there were other times he went apart
To pray, and by enduring FAITH—he won!

A SUGGESTION TO THE READER

While each of the three volumes of this Lincoln Trilogy is complete in itself and can be read without reference to any of the others, it may be that the reader's pleasure, appreciation and convenience will be increased by reference to the following features found only in Volume One.

THE GENERAL INTRODUCTION to this Lincoln Trilogy, *vol. I, pp. xvii-xxvii,* includes a brief history of the biographic sonnet sequence literary form, and tells of its authentication and enthusiastic acceptance by critics, biographers and average readers, as the most effective form in which to make possible this briefer, yet complete and dramatic, re-telling of our American epic—the life and character development of Abraham Lincoln.

THE ACKNOWLEDGEMENTS, *vol. I, pp. ix-xv,* gives specific reasons for the deep gratitude and indebtedness which the author of this Lincoln Trilogy owes to the following authors, editors, historians, character-forming educators and pastors; literary critics; legislators and friends: Dr. Allan Nevins, Dr. Marion Dolores Pratt, Dr. Benjamin P. Thomas, Dr. Herman B. Wells, Dr. Charles H. Coleman, Otto R. Kyle and Dr. Louis A. Warren; Dr. Van Chandler, Clarence O. and Marie L. Adams, Margaret Swett Mansfield, Mary O'Connor, Dr. Clement Wood and William Sharp; Congressman William L. Springer; and others too numerous to mention here.

THE BIBLIOGRAPHY, *vol. I, following p. 177,* lists books, periodicals, word- and picture-biographies, collections and critiques of Lincoln's speeches and prose and poetic writings, and other source materials such as certain books on historical, genealogical and religious backgrounds, which have been especially helpful to the author in the writing of this Lincoln Trilogy. Not all of these are cited as documentation in each volume's Addenda Notes.

CONTENTS

The Making of a Man: PREFACE TO VOLUME TWO 5
INTRODUCTION 15

LINCOLN GROWS IN LEARNING AND IN SERVICE

On His Own, March, 1831 21
The Hanks-Offutt Agreement, March, 1831 22
New Salem Meets Lincoln 23
New Orleans Slave Market, 1831 24
New Salem Adds a Store, September, 1831 25
Lincoln Keeps Store and Votes, August-September, 1831 ... 26
"Honest Abe" 27
The Clary's Grove Boys 28
Lincoln's Thirst for Knowledge 29
On Seeing Kirkham's Grammar, 1931 30
New Salem Folk 31
A Candidate for the Legislature, March 9, 1832 32
The Black Hawk War, April-June, 1832 33
Lincoln Loses the Election, 1832 34
Lincoln-Berry Store, January 15, 1833 35
Postmaster Lincoln, 1833-1836 36
Lincoln's First Court Case, 1833 37
The Classics 38
Pioneer Grace 39
Blackstone 40
Lincoln, Deputy Surveyor 41

7

Lincoln Runs for Assembly Again	42
Lincoln Learns to Debate, 1836-1837	43
Lincoln, the Legislator	44
Political Adolescence	45
Lincoln and Ann Rutledge, 1832	46
Abe Befriends Ann, 1834	47
Rutledge Reverses, About 1834	48
Death Enters, August 25, 1835	49
Ann's Burial, August 26, 1835	50
Grief Lost in Effort, 1836-1837	51
The Internal Improvements Bill, 1836-1837	52
The Long Nine	53
Lincoln Moves to Springfield, April, 1837	54
Stuart and Lincoln, Lawyers, April, 1837	55
Springfield, Capital of Illinois, 1839	56
Springfield's Social Life	57
Rewards of Effort, 1839-1841	58
Electoral College Candidate, 1838-1840	59
On the Circuit, 1839-1859	60
Circuit Courts, 1839	61
Lincoln Meets Mary Todd, 1839	62
The One Reality	63
Objections	64
Introspection	65
"The Fatal First of Jan'y"—1841	66
Logan and Lincoln, April 1841-December 1844	67
The Estrangement, 1841	68
Irish Ire, 1842	69
Love is Eternal, November 4, 1842	70
The Honeymoon	71
The Stork's Visit, August 1, 1843	72
Lincoln Buys a Home, 1844	73
Edward Baker Lincoln, March 10, 1846	74

LINCOLN SERVES THE PEOPLE AND A CAUSE

Lincoln Runs for Congress, 1846	77
Mrs. Sprigg's Boardinghouse, 1847	78
The Spot Resolution, December 22, 1847	79
Growing Conflict	80
Condemnation	81
Mary Visits Lexington, 1848-1849	82
Letters and Plaid Stockings, April 16, 1848	83
Second Year in Congress, 1848-1849	84
Lincoln and His Contemporaries, 1848-1849	85
"Gone Tapila"—1848	86
Lincoln's Social Standing, Congress, 1848	87
Death of John Quincy Adams, 1848	88
When Congress Closed, 1849	89
Had Lincoln Failed?—1847-1851	90
Back on the Circuit, 1840-1858	91
Circuit Reveries, 1850	92
Lincoln's Character Growth, 1849-1852	93
Moultrie County Circuit Court, 1852	94
"Uncle Bobby"—1852	95
"My Son, James"—1852	96
Family Ties, 1849	97
Lincoln and the Law, 1859	98
Relaxation	99
"Of Such is the Kingdom of Heaven"—February 1, 1850	100
The Christmas Gift, December 21, 1850	101
Death of Tom Lincoln, January 17, 1851	102
Stumbling Blocks	103
Lincoln's Sacrifice, January 17, 1851	104
The Missouri Compromise, 1820	105
Little Tad Lincoln, April 4, 1853	106
Kansas-Nebraska Act, 1854	107

Missouri Compromise Repeal, 1854 108
Back in Politics, 1854 109
The Lost Speech, May 29, 1856 110
Lincoln Enters the Senatorial Race, 1854-1855 111
Lincoln and Industry, 1850-1860 112
Lincoln and the West 113
Lincoln's Legal Expansion, 1857 114
McCormick-Manny Case, Cincinnati, 1854 115
Lincoln Chivalry, 1854 116
Republican Party Organized, May 29, 1856 117
Duff Armstrong's Trial, 1858 118
Lincoln Addresses the Jury, 1858 119
How Lincoln's Reputation Grew 120
A Full Year—"Judge" Lincoln, 1856 121
Lincoln Voted Senatorial Candidate, June 16, 1856 122
The Great Debate, 1852-1858 123
Political Forensic Giants, 1858 124
Douglas Travels in Style 125
The People are Aroused, 1858 126
The Freeport Doctrine, August, 1858 127
Victory in Defeat, 1858 128

LINCOLN BECOMES LEADER OF A DIVIDING PEOPLE

The Lincoln Philosophy 131
A Late Autumnal Walk, November, 1858 132
Retrieving Loss, November, 1858 133
Lincoln Discovered, 1859 134
Henry Ward Beecher's Invitation 135
At Cooper Union, February 27, 1860 136
The Cooper Union Speech, February 27, 1860 137
Recognized Leadership, 1860 138

Table of Contents

Events Can Create a President, August 8, 1860	139
"Lincoln, the Rail-Splitter"—May 9-10, 1860	140
Presidential Candidate, May 10, 1860	141
National Republican Convention, May 16-18, 1860, Chicago	142
Lincoln Nominated for President, May 18, 1860, Chicago	143
Lincoln Officially Notified, May 19, 1860	144
Republican Platform, 1860	145
Lincoln's Loyal Friends	146
Democratic National Convention, 1860	147
Lincoln's State House Office, Summer, 1860	148
Campaign Irony	149
Campaign Demonstrations, 1860	150
Springfield Rally, August 8, 1860	151
A Pledge of Loyalty, August 8, 1860	152
Election Day, November 6, 1860	153
"Mary, We Have Won!"	154
Secession Begins, December 20, 1860	155
Lincoln Visits His Stepmother, January 31, 1861	156
Treason Stalked the Land, February 4, 1861	157
Lincoln's Last Walk	158
Lincoln Senses His Task, February, 1861	159
The Great Western Station, February 11, 1861	160
"An Affectionate Farewell"—February 11, 1861	161
The Train Leaves Springfield, 8:20 A.M., February 11, 1861	162
On Lincoln's Inaugural Train	163
Nearing Decatur, 9:24 A.M.	164
Decatur Strong for Lincoln	165
A Man of Friends	166
Mary Lincoln Rebels	167
Gist of Lincoln's Speech Enroute	168
Plot and Counterplot	169
Lincoln Reaches Washington, February 23, 1861	170
"The Lincoln Special" Arrives	171

ABRAHAM LINCOLN: THE MAN

President Buchanan Receives 172
Planning the Inauguration 173
Night Before Inauguration, March 3, 1861 174

ADDENDA NOTES 175

INDEX 189

LIST OF ILLUSTRATIONS

Abraham Lincoln—Congressman-elect	14a
Lincoln's 1831 Flatboat	14b
Rutledge Tavern Dining Room	14b
New Salem's Main Street	14b
Offutt's Mill and Store	14b
Indian Chief Black Hawk	14b
The Lincoln-Berry Store	14b
Mentor Graham	14c
Sarah Bush Lincoln	14c
(No authentic pictures of Thomas or Nancy Lincoln are available)	
Major John Todd Stuart	14c
Joshua Fry Speed	14c
Mary Todd Lincoln	14c
Reverend Charles Dresser	14c
Judge Stephen Trigg Logan	14c
Senator Stephen A. Douglas	14c
Judge David Davis	14c
Stuart-Lincoln Law Office	14d
Log Court House at Decatur	14d
Lincoln on the Circuit	14d
Abe Pleads with "Duff" Armstrong Jury	14d
Lincoln-Herndon Law Office	14d
Moultrie County Court House, 1852	14d
Mary Todd's Home in Springfield	14e
Globe Tavern, Home of Lincoln Newlyweds	14e
Lincoln's Story-and-a-Half 8th St. Home	14e
First Presbyterian Church, Springfield	14e
Little Eddie Lincoln's Tombstone	14e

14   ABRAHAM LINCOLN: THE MAN

Captain Lincoln of Black Hawk War 14f
Congressman Lincoln Telling Jokes at Dinner 14f
Mrs. Mary Lincoln and Willie and Tad Lincoln 14f
Lincoln at Time of Cooper Union Address 14f
Lincoln-Douglas Debate at Charleston 14g
State House at Vandalia 14g
State House at Springfield 14g
Republican Wigwam in Chicago, 1860 .... 14g
Lincoln Awaits Reports at Telegraph Office 14h
Springfield Rally at Lincoln's Home 14h
Gavel Made from "Lincoln-Hewn" Fence Rail 14h
Committee Notifies Lincoln of Nomination 14h
Rear Platform Farewell to Springfield 14h

MAPS AND SURVEYS

Lincoln Square, Decatur, Illinois 20
Map of New Salem, Illinois 20
Map of Illinois and Michigan Territory 32a
    (Charts: Flatboat Trip, Black Hawk War, Judicial Circuit,
                        Lincoln-Douglas Debates)
Lincoln's Survey Map of Albany, Illinois 40a
Map of 1837 Illinois Internal Improvements 51a
Lincoln's Social Standing Survey: Cotillion Invitation 51a

ILL. STATE HIST. LIBRARY

CONGRESSMAN-ELECT ABRAHAM LINCOLN

This daguerreotype made in 1846, now in the Library of Congress, is the earliest known photograph of Illinois' self-made frontier lawyer, then Congressman-elect.

But twelve years later he was to mark himself as a national figure by declaring in his acceptance speech as a U. S. Senate nominee, "a house divided against itself cannot stand." Though defeated for the Senate, his campaign debates with brilliant orator-incumbent Stephen A. Douglas gave Lincoln national prominence. In 1860, his scholarly address at Cooper Union in New York led to his becoming President-elect.

Black Hawk: ILL. STATE HIST. LIBRARY. Others: UNIV. OF ILL. LIBRARY

NEW SALEM IN LINCOLN'S TIME

Upper, l. to r. — (1) Lincoln's 1831 flatboat stuck on the milldam at New Salem. (2) Rutledge Tavern dining room where Abe and John McNeil (McNamar) ate, and where they each met Ann Rutledge. (3) Main street in the village of New Salem. *Lower, l. to r.* — (4) Sangamon river milldam, and the mill and (just beyond Clary's Grocery on the bluff above) Offut's store, where Abe first worked in New Salem. (5) Black Hawk, as in 1833 the artist Charles B. King portrayed this Indian Chief against whom Lincoln soldiered as a captain. (6) The Lincoln and Berry store.

ILL. STATE HIST. LIBRARY

A FEW WHO INFLUENCED LINCOLN'S LIFE

Upper, l. to r. — (1) Mentor Graham, tutor who advised him to study *Kirkham's Grammar*. (2) Sarah Bush Lincoln, step-mother who encouraged his interest in learning. (3) Major John Todd Stuart, who urged him to study law, loaned him books, and was his first law partner. *Center, l. to r.* — (4) Joshua Fry Speed, wealthy Springfield merchant who became his most intimate friend. (5) Mary Todd Lincoln, his wife (from 1846 daguerreotype in Library of Congress). (6) Rev. Charles Dresser, who read his marriage vows and sold him his home. *Lower, l. to r.* — (7) Judge Stephen Trigg Logan, his second law partner, with whom he became a leading lawyer in Illinois. (8) Stephen Arnold Douglas, his rival in love and politics. (9) Judge David Davis, his companion on the Circuit and chief strategist in securing his nomination as President. (No authentic photos of Tom and Nancy Lincoln are available.)

Center left: ILL. STATE HIST. LIBRARY. *Others:* UNIV. OF ILL. LIBRARY

LINCOLN AS A LAWYER

Upper, l. to r. — (1) His law office with Stuart was on the second floor of this building. (2) Old log courthouse in Decatur, where he had some of his earliest law cases. *Center, l. to r.* — (3) At first, bad roads and weather often made it necessary to travel the Circuit on horseback, carrying his legal papers in his high hat — as he had done the mail when New Salem's postmaster. (4) He pleads with the jury as he defends "Duff" Armstrong, on trial for murder. *Lower, l. to r.* — (5) His law office with Herndon was on the second floor of the third building from the corner. (6) The Moultrie County courthouse, as it appeared in 1852 when he knew "Uncle Bobby" Crowder and his son, James.

LINCOLN COURTS AND WEDS MARY TODD

Upper, l. to r. — (1) Springfield home of Mary Todd, where she lived with Ninian Edwards, her guardian, and his wife, her sister, and where she and Lincoln were wed. (2) Globe Tavern (1865 photo), where the Lincoln newlyweds roomed and boarded for four dollars a week, and where their first child, Robert, was born. *Lower, l. to r.* — (3) Their 1½ story home on Eighth Street, before its full second story was added. Here Eddie, Willie and Tad were born and Eddie died. (4) Springfield's First Presbyterian Church, which the Lincolns attended, and whose pastor conducted Eddie's funeral. (5) Eddie's tombstone, inscribed: "Of such is the kingdom of heaven."

Left two: ILL. STATE HIST. LIBRARY. *Right two:* UNIV. OF ILL. LIBRARY

LINCOLN CONTRASTS AND ABSENTEES

Upper, l. to r. — (1) Captain Lincoln of the Black Hawk War, as sculptor Leonard Crunelle has portrayed him in his statue at Dixon, Ill. (2) Congressman Lincoln as he covered up his loneliness, during the absence of his wife and boys, by telling jokes and stories at dinner in Mrs. Sprigg's boarding-house across from the Capitol in Washington. *Lower, l. to r.* — (3) Mary Lincoln and their two boys, having found boarding-house life cramped, had gone for a visit with Grandpa Todd in Lexington, Ky. (4) Orator Lincoln when, at Cooper Union in 1860, he was soon to be President-elect.

Top & center r: ILL. STATE HIST. LIBRARY. *Others:* UNIV. OF ILL. LIBRARY

LINCOLN'S STEPS TO THE PRESIDENCY

Upper — (1) The Lincoln-Douglas debate at Charleston, wherein artist Robert M. Root shows Lincoln standing and his inveterate rival, incumbent Senator Douglas, seated by the table on Lincoln's right. *Center, l. to r.* — (2) State House at Vandalia, where he served his political adolescence as, usually, leader of the "Long Nine." (3) State House at Springfield, where he made his famous "House Divided" speech and, later, had his office as President-elect, before going to Washington. *Lower* — (4) Republican Wigwam in Chicago, 1860, where Norman Judd nominated him for the Presidency.

Top l. & r.: Univ. of Ill. Library. *Others*: Chicago Hist. Society Dioramas

CANDIDATE LINCOLN, ELECTED PRESIDENT, LEAVES FOR WASHINGTON

Upper, l. to r. — (1) Telegraph office where he awaited reports, first, of his nomination, and then, election as President. (2) His two-story home on Eighth Street, during the Springfield rally when canes made from "Lincoln-hewn" rails were handed out to participants. (3) Gavel made from one of those canes, which Mt. Zion Academy student, James H. Crowder, received from Lincoln's own hand. *Lower, l. to r.* — (4) The Committee, received in Lincoln's parlor, as they notified him of his nomination for the Presidency. (5) President-elect Lincoln, on the rear platform of the train at the Great Western station, as he bade "affectionate farewell" to his Springfield friends before leaving for Washington.

INTRODUCTION

It has been said that among the great men of modern history, there is no one who ranks higher than Abraham Lincoln. The life story of this man is an inspiration to all who read it. It stands as a monument to his memory, and as a receipt for other men's success. It reveals to the young man or woman—who may be dreaming dreams and building air castles for the morrow—ways and means of attaining them. It illuminates the path of the struggler who may be already in the field beset by trials and defeats, and it convinces him that *trials are but tests* to prove his worthiness of success.

There is perhaps no period in Lincoln's life which reveals more clearly his many continuous discouragements than in that which is recorded in *Volume II* of this Lincoln Trilogy. Here, also, we find his methods of overcoming disheartening difficulties. It was in this period— between his twenty-second and fifty-second years—that he proved *WHO he was.*

These were the years when his mind and body were building wisdom, intellect and power, when the significance of living was becoming forever deeply impressed upon him. These were years in which he learned that the life breath within him was *never born,* and *can never die*

—that earthly "life is but a sojourn between two eternities."

It was in these years that he married and became the father of four sons, which added to his responsibility and *need* to succeed. And it was during these years that death stepped in and robbed him of two of his loved ones, his little son, Eddie, and his father, Thomas Lincoln. The shock sustained in the loss of these dear ones tore at the foundations of his faith until he came to realize more fully his relationship to the All-Powerful, Ever-Present and Ever-Ruling Divine, to whom all men owe allegiance and can always turn for comfort and guidance.

It was during these years that—while using many other callings to gain his ends—he chose the Law profession as his life work, and mastered it so completely that he became known as one of the leading attorneys in Illinois. And it was while traveling the Eighth Judicial Circuit, as a practicing attorney, that he met the people of Illinois and they came to know, love and trust him. Thus it was that they gladly elected him to represent them in their interests, both in the State Assembly and in the Congress of the United States.

It was during these years that he came to be known as "a man of mystery," because of his marvelous intellectual and cultural growth. Indeed, few then or since, were able to understand this mystic power. But its tremendous impact was so pronounced in his speech and writing that his friends urged him to challenge Stephen A. Douglas—

then known as the nation's greatest orator—for a series of debates, which Douglas accepted and the national newspapers broadcast all over the country.

Great throngs attended these seven debates which lifted Lincoln to national prominence. He was thereafter called east and west in recognition of his ability as a speaker, and was acclaimed a profound thinker and reasoner. Ultimately, at the age of fifty-one, he was named, nominated and elected President of the United States.

No college bells had rung out the praises of Abraham Lincoln, nor was this—his election to the nation's highest office—*a gift* of the people, for all were cognizant of his lifelong struggles whereby *he had well earned* their trust. They knew, too, that their country was then *in need* of his master judgment, his unequaled wisdom and his understanding, sympathetic heart, for they realized that this great man had learned—by the mastery of his own difficulties—how to master those of his beloved Republic, when all was discord and war seemed imminent.

D. C. M.

LINCOLN

GROWS

IN LEARNING AND IN SERVICE

Upper: By Gerald Puckette.

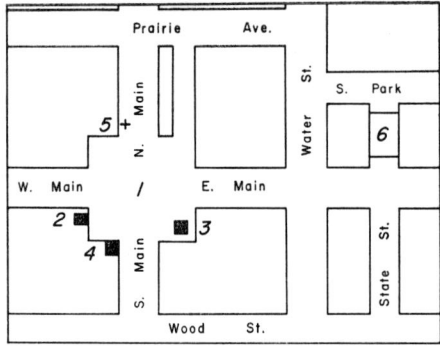

Lower: Univ. of Ill. Library.

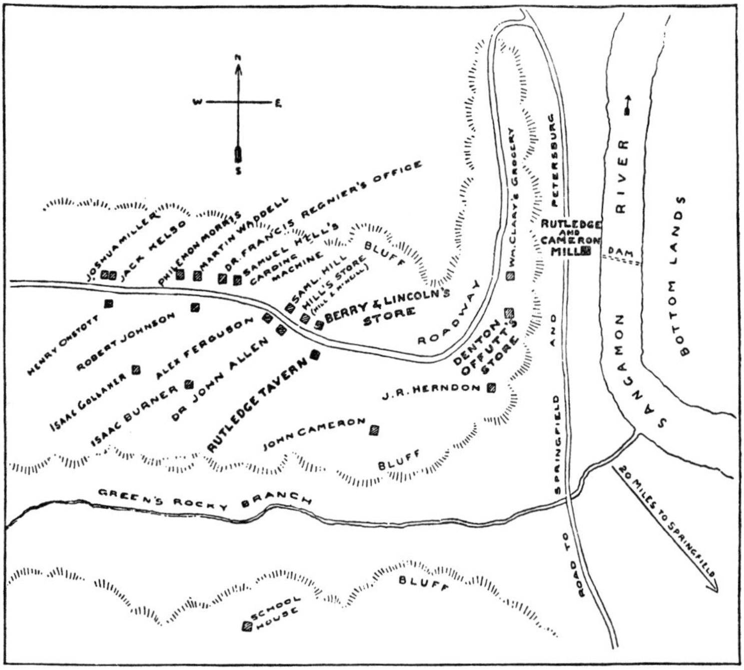

Upper: (1) Lincoln Square, Decatur, Ill. where the Lincoln caravan stopped in front of the then unfinished log courthouse on their arrival in 1830. (2) Site of log courthouse, scene of Lincoln law cases, May, 1838. (3) Site of brick courthouse, scene of Lincoln law cases in Decatur after 1838. (4) Site of the Cassell House where, in 1856, Lincoln first allied himself with anti-Nebraska editors' conference, forerunner of the Republican Party in Illinois. (5) Site of Renshaw's store in front of which Lincoln, in 1830, made his first political speech in Illinois. (6) Site of Republican State Convention wigwam in 1860. *Lower:* Map of New Salem, Ill. where, 1831-1837, as mill and store clerk, surveyor and postmaster, Lincoln read law and was elected to State Legislature.

Abraham Lincoln: The Man

ON HIS OWN
March, 1831

And now that seeds are sown we must await
The growth of fibrous roots that reach and claw
Their life and strength from out the earth's broad maw,
While greening limbs stretch wide and tall to mate
With sun and sky. Abe's growth was slow, but straight;
His wisdom towers through justice, right and law.
These, with his love of men, have left small flaw
To mend, while faith and courage are innate.

Ambition's view is dim, the distant goal
Is bleared by hardship's test—at every turn
His urge to reach encounters hidden shoal;
But such perfects his struggling will to earn
High leadership. Thus rose the Lincoln soul—
Through fogs that blind, and flames that leap and burn.

THE HANKS-OFFUTT AGREEMENT
March, 1831

"Now, Abe, when yo' folks go, yo'll be alone,"*
John† said, "so, Offutt thought 'fore things turns green,
'at yo's would steer his boat to ol' Orleen.
Spring markets now air high, an' they'll be prone
T' need our garden stuff that we have grown:
Our taters, pork, dried fruit and flour 'at's clean.
I'll stick along t' he'p yo' git thar 'tween
Late March an' May—'twill hurry us, I own.

"I's got a big canoe[1] t' take us down
The Sangamon, for roads air flooded bad
Ag'in. We'll start at dawn for Springfield town—
'at's whar Dent Offutt is." But Offutt had
No boat, till Abe and Hanks made one of brown,
Tough wood. Then Offutt§ cried, "Heave off, my lad!"

---

* Words of conversation and dialect, attributed to a speaker in this Trilogy, are usually not intended as a direct quote, but are merely a narrative portrayal of the manner, facts and spirit of the times, events and persons concerned.

† John Hanks, Lincoln's cousin.

§ Denton Offutt was a buyer and shipper of farm produce. John Johnston, Lincoln's stepbrother, accompanied Abe to New Orleans. But, because of the six-week delay while having to make the boat, John Hanks went with Abe only as far as St. Louis and returned home to put in his crops.[2]

NEW SALEM MEETS LINCOLN

The flatboat clung to sands till rail and oar
Had pushed it free, then shot on down midstream
To ride the deeper waves that dance and gleam.
For miles the cargo skimmed the water's floor,
Until around a bend was heard the roar
Of small New Salem's dam. The flat, abeam
The dam, then stuck! No means to free—or scheme—
Would work, that was proposed by men on shore.

The water swamped the boat and Lincoln knew
It had to be removed, and so he drilled
A hole to let it out!* The flat lunged through,
And drifted on. And Lincoln's genius thrilled
The men who watched and shouted wild halloo,
Because they saw his mind and hands were skilled.

---

* Lincoln shifted the cargo until the water ran out, then he plugged up the hole and the flat was lightened enough to clear the dam.[3] *See map, p. 20, this volume.*

NEW ORLEANS SLAVE MARKET
1831

Abe walked again New Orleans' cobblestone,
Gray-aged and rough, where garrish women smiled
And beckoned him and drunken sailors whiled
Their time. He heard strange speech, unlike his own,
And witnessed sales of human flesh and bone.
He saw brash notices of slave girls, styled
As *chic!* " 'Give me a chance,' " Abe said, well riled
And sad, " 'I'll hit that hard.'*—They must atone!"

Abe sold the cargo and the flatboat too,
Then said, "Come, John,† we must be getting on
To give report to Offutt at Saint Lou;
We'll take this steamer here—it leaves at dawn."§
And Offutt was well pleased and said, "Abe, you
Can clerk for me—I like your brain and brawn."

---

* This statement, in quote marks within quote marks, is purported by various authors to express, in substance, Lincoln's impression.

† John Johnston.

§ The actual trip down the river and back took about three months. Lincoln was back by July (1831), and at that time visited his father on the Buck Grove farm in western Coles County.[4] *See map, p. 32a, this volume.*

NEW SALEM ADDS A STORE
September, 1831

"While Abe and John are down there at Orleens,"
Dent Offutt mused, "I'll buy, at Old Saint Lou,
Some dry goods for a store—food staples too,
Including dishes, rice and army beans.
But now—just where'll I put that store? Ravines
Make easy trails . . . New Salem,* with its few
Choice settlers, is the best place I've gone through;
Its friendly folks have lures, as have its scenes.

"An' Abe . . . his talent, whims an' jokes will draw
Much trade. I'll mention it when comes the day
For his return . . . I think most certainly
He'l take the store an' manage it . . . Though raw
And much unschooled, his genius finds a way;
With Abe I'm safe . . . Yes, Abe's the man for me!"†

---

* ". . . in this place he [Lincoln] was to equip himself for the successive roles which he should play as politician, lawyer, statesman, and martyr. . ."[5]

† Lincoln was to receive $15 per month and privilege to sleep in a back room, for being clerk in charge of store and mill.[6]

LINCOLN KEEPS STORE AND VOTES
August-September, 1831

When Offutt's store had opened full display
Of wares,* young Abe unbarred the door and found
The needy settlers there from miles around.
He met their many wants and took as pay
A hog, a cow, some eggs or load of hay.
They liked him, liked his mirth as he unwound
Some poplin for the girls who go well-gowned,
Or apron prints, or dipped up rice to weigh.

Election time, Abe cast his first known vote.†
The poll was held at Cameron's.§ Much fun
And wit prevailed, for Abe was always strong
On jokes and quips and thrilling anecdote;
He kept the crowd amused till set of sun,
And all those joy-filled hours they treasured long.

---

* Sometime in September, after its supplies had finally arrived.

† August 1, 1831. Since the store had not yet opened, Abe was free and so spent the day at the election poll[7] getting acquainted with his prospective customers.

§ John Cameron's house, where Lincoln boarded.

"HONEST ABE"

As Abe kept Offutt's store his friendships grew;
New Salem gave him welcome far and near,
And settlers from remotest parts would hear
His fame and come to swap the wit they knew.
The work there kept him busy and but few
Could know he worked at night to fairly clear
His books and balance sales with costs, to steer
His business honestly the long months through.

One night, Abe saw the intake of the store
Had totaled six cents higher than was fair.
He searched and found the error, closed the door,
And walked three miles to pay the debtor's share.
The woman owed cried, "Honest Abe!" Now, lore
And legend still extol his noble flair.

THE CLARY'S GROVE BOYS

Dent Offutt praised Abe's brawn. "I know," said he,
"Abe's wrestling beats the best—been licked by none!"
The Clary gang's conceit urged on the fun
And challenged Abe a wrestling bout, to see
If Abe could meet Jack Armstrong's prowessy.
The day soon came, the wrestling had begun:
It, first, was tit for tat—Jack almost won;
Then Abe seized him and threw him bodily.

The gang jumped in; Abe stood against the wall.
"Now, boys," Abe called, "if any want to fight,
I'll take you—each alone!" Then came Jack's bawl:
"Come, boys, hands off; Abe's winner square an' right!"
Jack shook Abe's hand and vowed with solemn drawl,
"Abe Lincoln, I admire your brawn and might."

LINCOLN'S THIRST FOR KNOWLEDGE

Abe knew his speech was dialectal, slow,
With drawl, and sought for Graham's remedy.
"A grammar* with its rules will help," said he,
"And rhetoric that everyone should know."
Abe got the book, and when the calico
And gingham sales had stopped, with no more tea
To weigh, Abe studied hard and came to see:
Correctness practiced daily makes speech grow.

When Mentor Graham saw Abe's thirst for books,
He lent him some that Abe had never read.
Abe's friends, in leisure hours, liked fishing hooks
And wrestling bouts and cock fights; but Abe said,
"I'll choose a book— What matters how it looks
Outside? I'll get what's in . . . till hunger's fed."

---

* Kirkham's Grammar.

ON SEEING KIRKHAM'S GRAMMAR
1931

So this book once was Lincoln's—touched his hand!
This book's pure syntax permeated through
His thought until his rhetoric was true!
This volume gave his speech and writing brand
Of exellence! Not many understand
How Abe, self-taught, acquired so much and grew
Until he mastered words by much review
And gained a perfect English at command.

O, Abe, your toil-worn hands once held this book!
We treasure it, and bless the memory
It brings: a tall lad reading by a brook
At sunset, straining eager eyes to see!
Now, lessons done, you rest in sculptured nook
Among the great of earth, triumphantly!

---

* *Kirkham's Grammar* was kept in the Lincoln Room of the Decatur Public Library for many years, but was sent to the Library of Congress in Washington, D. C., on February 13, 1932.

NEW SALEM FOLK

New Salem* folk could not forget the man
Whose talents proved a special quality†
Not found in all. They were most glad to see
Abe put in charge of Offutt's store, with plan
To share mill tasks.[8] New Salem's leading clan
Was English—same as Lincoln's pedigree—
And knowing well that fruit from one big tree
Would taste the same, endorsement soon began.

With Kelso, Rutledge, Cameron and Hill,
Doc Allen, Graham, Rankin—sure but slow,
And all the Clary boys—who joked at will,
Squire Green, Smoot, Short and Berry to bestow
A needful service in some craft or skill,
No finer class could Lincoln come to know.

---

* New Salem consisted of a blacksmith shop, two mills, three stores, a church which also served as a schoolhouse, and at least six or seven dwellings.

† New Salem folk well remembered Abe's ingenious method which he had used to get the flatboat over their dam.

A CANDIDATE FOR THE LEGISLATURE
March 9, 1832

Abe read George Washington's biography
When young—not yet quite ten.* It left an urge
In Lincoln's mind for truthfulness to surge
Through him, as in great men—inspired and free,
But firm and strong for our Democracy.
Big parties were contending in their splurge
For leadership, forecast of later purge
That awed the world.† This, Lincoln sensed to be.

Abe entered politics with this in view,
To represent his party and his state:
"I stand for waterways, well opened through
To markets; better schools, and lower rate
Of interest on loans. Now, I am new,
But seek to serve as your one candidate."

---

* Weems' *Life of Washington*.

† Thirty-three years later, after the three leading parties in the North had united to form the Republican party, the world was awed by what that party achieved in fighting the Civil War, and purging the nation of slavery.

Univ. of Ill. Library — Added routes by Gerald Puckette.

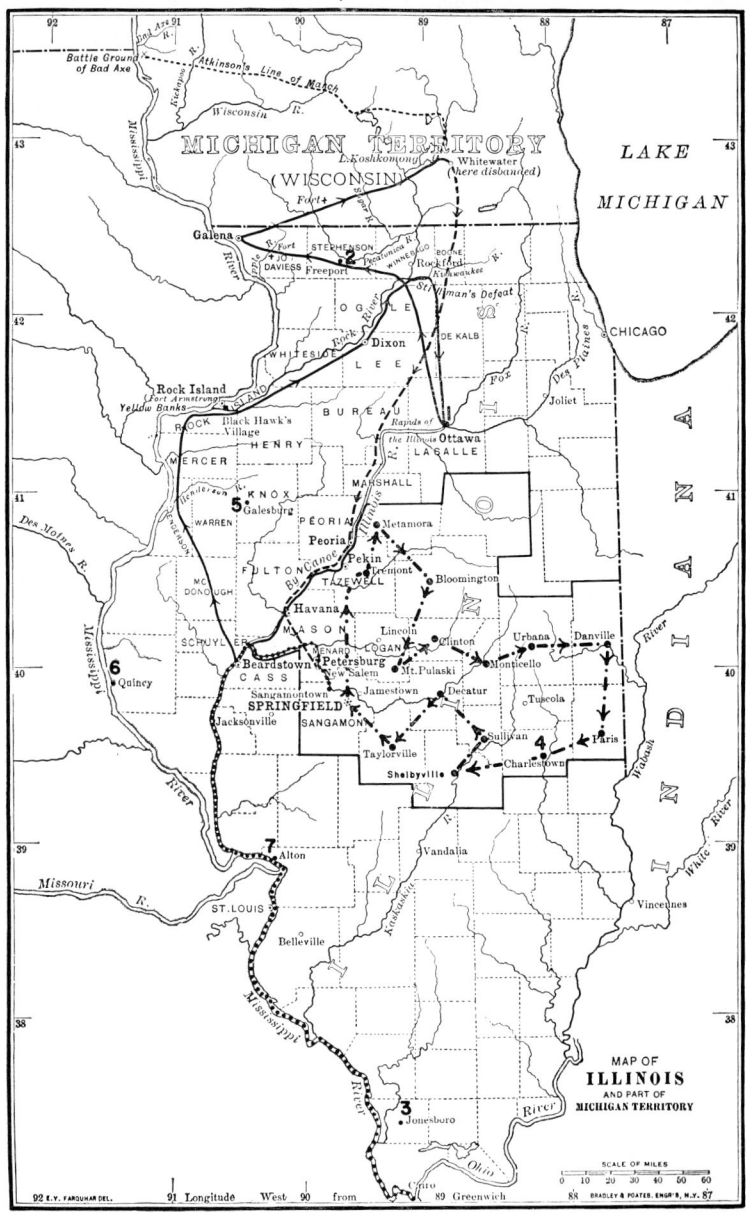

The above map shows: (a) *In dot-line,* route of Lincoln's flatboat trip from Sangamontown, past New Salem, and on to New Orleans in 1831. (b) *In solid-, and dash-line,* Lincoln's route to, and from, the Black Hawk War. (c) *In dot-and-dash-line,* Lincoln's route to countyseats on Eighth Judicial Circuit as established by law of 1847. (d) The seven Lincoln-Douglas debates are numbered in the order of their occurrence at the towns indicated thereby.

THE BLACK HAWK WAR
April-June, 1832

About mid-April eighteen thirty-two,
A mud-bespattered rider came to town
With news that old Black Hawk, with savage frown
And knife, was scalping settlers whom he knew
Had no defense.* "Swift steeds bring riders through,
When dark, to burn the settlers' cabins down.
Four hundred men, enlisted now, may drown
These fires of warrior hate that thus ensue."

Abe heard the crier and resolved to write
His name† as one to stand for Illinois;[9]
Jack Armstrong guessed Abe's mind to join the fray,
And all the Clary gang signed up. That night
They chose Abe captain, and with hope and joy,
And bugles blowing, bravely marched away.

---

* The Sauk and Fox Indians, dissatisfied with their land in Iowa, had re-crossed the Mississippi to put out their crops on the Illinois side. Panic spread among the settlers. Someone started shooting, and the Indians retaliated by burning the settlers' cabins down.

† Lincoln was in the service for about three months.

LINCOLN LOSES THE ELECTION
1832

Election was but eighteen days away
When Abe returned from war. This time he spent
In making speeches where he could, and lent
A hand to farmers—helped them store their hay
And cradle wheat, refusing proffered pay.
Men learned his politics was sound. Anent
Their views, he strove his best to represent;
And Springfield heard him near election day.*

But Abe placed eighth of thirteen candidates,[10]
Though in his own precinct the vote was won
By full nine tenths; in fact, he thought the gates
Would open yet to him, that work begun
Would grow as it does unto him who waits
In preparation for the course to run.

---

* Lincoln spoke in Springfield on August 4th.

LINCOLN-BERRY STORE
January 15, 1833

Since cash was low, Abe looked quite fervently
For honest work to earn his needful due.
One told him carpenters were hired for two
Or maybe five a day in coin. The fee
Was bait, but Law was lure—though Abe could see
Such choice demanded bookish grind in lieu
Of hard hand toil. He bought a store,* yet knew
Small interest in selling jeans and tea.

Abe read law books, neglected sales, while trout
Lured Berry fishing, which made both decide
There were too many stores—so theirs "'winked out,'"†
And Abe assumed the debt when Berry died!§
For years it was a load on Abe to rout,
But every cent was paid with honest pride!

---

* William F. Berry, former partner of Rowan Herndon, agreed to let Herndon sell his interest in the store to Lincoln on credit.[11]

† Lincoln's own words.[12] (When in this Trilogy's sonnets, use is made of the *actual words* of Lincoln, they are *set in quote marks within quote marks* and documented.)

§ William F. Berry died January 10th, 1835 and Lincoln was left with a debt of $1,100 which he laughingly called "the National Debt."[13]

POSTMASTER LINCOLN
1833-1836

New Salem's postmaster was Samuel Hill,
Who irked the women of the town by sheer
Neglect of distribution. So severe
Their need for change, they felt an urgent will
To break the gyve, petitioning a bill
To Washington; expressing hopes sincere,
They wrote: "Abe Lincoln is the man out here
To have this post, and he can ably fill."

One day in spring, Abe was appointed there.*
He donned his stovepipe hat, from which much fame
Has come, and carried in its lofty care
The mail for those down sick, or ones too lame
To come—for Lincoln's heart, benign to share,
Served everyone as friend without acclaim.

---

* Lincoln was appointed postmaster at New Salem, May 7, 1833 and served until May 30, 1836, when the office was moved to Petersburg.[14]

LINCOLN'S FIRST COURT CASE
1833

In sunset hours Abe followed turns and crooks
Along some stream or trail through woodland scent,
To rest where sunlight's gold was prevalent
To light the pages of some statute books,
Or tomes on pleading. There, in quiet nooks,
He read till sun was gone and light was spent.
Then Abe would plead aloud case argument—
Heard only by the frogs and babbling brooks.

Squire Bowling Green was Abe's good counselor,
Explaining statutes of the state to him;
In lower court he let Abe try a case
Without a fee. Sometimes they would concur.*
In time Abe came to glimpse a star; though dim,
It scintillated there in future space!

---

* In order to teach procedure to Lincoln, the good Squire would often work a case through with him.[15]

THE CLASSICS

On days when mail arrived, all could rely
On Abe's delivery. Then, evening's glow
Would bring his blacksmith friend‡ to urge he go
With him through forest glades, for Jack would sigh:
"Come, Abe, let's both go fishin'—nothin' I
Can do that rests me more than sprawl below
On river bank, or drift in skiff with toe,*
Yet not the fish to seek, but woods and sky.

"For there we sense a kinship as we quote
Some homey lines from Burns or Bill Shakespeare.
'How sweet the moonlight sleeps,'† Bill thought and
    wrote;
It sleeps to heal man's ills from nerve-wrought gear!
'To see oursels as others see us'—note,
Burns said—frees us 'frae mony a blunder' here"§

---

‡ Jack Kelso.
* A line with several hooks on it tied to a skiff or rowboat.
† William Shakespeare, *Merchant of Venice,* Act V, Scene 1.
§ Robert Burns, "To a Louse," stanza 8.

PIONEER GRACE

New Salem's social life was typed *frontier,*
Yet everyone with open eyes could see
There lived and thrived a social nicety
Of custom, with which each should try to gear
His own response. Abe sensed his lacks and fear,
And strove for poise to set his body free;
Then flashed his mother's words from memory:
"It's heart, not dress, that makes of man a peer!"

Too many writers have declared his days—
His early ones—were those of want. Abe knew
No lack, but lived with hero's will the ways
That men who ride the nation's van pursue:
A life of labor with one's hands, to blaze
Out timber trails, that *others* may come through.

BLACKSTONE

Abe learned the great importance of one book
To which all legal texts would constantly
Refer as source. He found no rest till he
Secured a copy. Though use-soiled, one look
Within that tome and you could never brook
A doubt as to the need of it—a key
To Common Law, in phraseology
That each wise lawyer stores in mental nook.

He read it while at his New Salem store,
As postmaster, or resting on survey.
He studied every case which all the more
Made evident its clarifying ray.
In mind, Abe argued cases by the score[*]
And visioned listeners his thoughts could sway.

[*] He developed procedure by arguing cases imaginatively, for he had had no aid in procedure aside from Squire Green's directing.

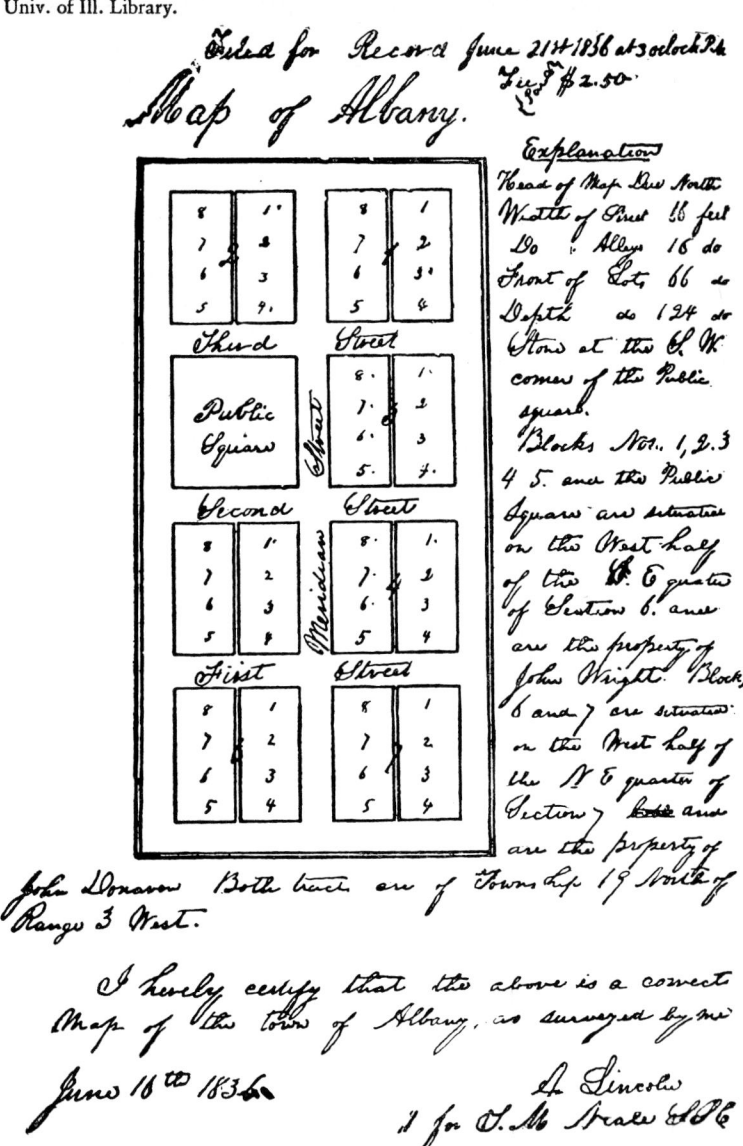

LINCOLN'S SURVEY MAP OF ALBANY, ILLINOIS

Note: The explanation, certification and signature of this survey map, dated **June** 10, 1836, are in *Lincoln's own handwriting*.

LINCOLN, DEPUTY SURVEYOR
1834

The state was filling rapidly with men
Who bought up farms which needed true survey
To fix dividing lines, stone-marked to stay.‡
With farms all fenced and trails blocked out, Abe then
Surveyed the wagon roads through hill and glen.
Thus given chance to earn much needed pay,
He borrowed books and studied night and day,
Good Mentor Graham lending aid again.

Calhoun, Surveyor of the County, said
His office lacked a steadfast deputy
And urged young Abe to take the job.* This led
Abe first, to Reason Shipley's farm,† then he
Went next to Russell Godbey's place. Days fled,
And other farms and towns§ came rapidly.

---

‡ Stones were used to mark the corners of each farm.

* *Lincoln himself says,* "He accepted, procured a compass and chain, studied Flint, and Gibson . . . and went at it."[16]

† 800 acres.[17]

§ The towns of Albany, Bath, Huron, New Boston and Petersburg were surveyed by Lincoln, and several roads which he surveyed are still in use.[18]

LINCOLN RUNS FOR ASSEMBLY AGAIN

In eighteen thirty-four Abe placed his name
Again as an Assembly candidate.
This was election only for the state
And lacked the nation's stronger contest flame.
With Lincoln's popularity the same
With Democrats and Whigs, friends urged, "Don't wait,
You'll surely win! No need to hesitate."
And Abe, on August fourth, did win the game.[19]

With doubtings at an end, Abe knew that law
Would now be first pursuit. Intrigued, he read
It night and day. His native bent, though raw,
Was pointing him to this resolve. He said,
"I'll borrow books to study!"* And his jaw
Went set: "I'll master it, and plunge ahead!"

---

* Lincoln borrowed books from Major John T. Stuart, whom he had met in the Black Hawk War and who was at this time a fellow-Assemblyman and attorney living in Springfield.[20]

LINCOLN LEARNS TO DEBATE
1836-1837

Abe's boyhood trends gave ample evidence
His mind could bear no ambiguity
In speech or written word. An inner plea
Would ponder thought with eager diligence
Till it was well expressed with eloquence,
Each subtle meaning shaded perfectly.
His analytic mind delved deep to be
Assured of speaking with pre-eminence.

To test their minds on issues of the day,
The Men's Debating Club* wrangled a lot
And urged Abe join. "Now, here's a chance to grow
In argument," thought Abe. "Each one I weigh
Will trace true meanings from the polyglot,
And thus, by such a practice, *I can know.*"

---

* The Men's Debating Society of New Salem.

LINCOLN, THE LEGISLATOR
1834-1835

November came and Abe bought clothes and went
By stage down to the capital of state.*
He learned how politicians operate
Behind the scenes; how lobbyists come bent
On seeing bills made law, at times intent
Upon some selfish scheme of power and weight.
He heard skilled statesmen argue and debate
For some good bill they thought was exigent.

He met† the rich, the poor, the brash, the rude,
Strong men of breeding, some of charm—a glim
Of higher education which brought food
To satisfy his hungering, and dim
His fears, his shyness and provincial mood,
With poise and courage as their antonym.

---

* Vandalia was then the capital of Illinois.

† One of those whom he met for the first time at Vandalia in 1835 was Stephen A. Douglas, who was four years younger than Lincoln.[21]

POLITICAL ADOLESCENCE

No contacts made by Abe had been so strong
To boost his growth as those he and a few
Men had observed in making laws go through.
He learned how politicians may go wrong,
And how, for right and justice, statesmen throng;
He noted well their differential view.
Though yet in adolescent stage, he knew
Much strife was sure, if *he* endured for long.

He planned and acted as associate
Of those who, like himself, were pioneers
Of trust to frame the laws and legislate
For settlers on the prairie land frontiers.
If they achieved but little for the State,
Great good was wrought for Lincoln's future years.

LINCOLN AND ANN RUTLEDGE
1832

McNeil and Abe ate at the tavern where
They met the pretty daughter, turned nineteen.
"Miss Ann" was chic and sweet, the village queen,
With big blue eyes and lovely auburn hair;
And everywhere Ann went, McNeil was there.
Some said they were engaged, but when the green
Returned with spring, McNeil was nowhere seen!*
Some said he jilted Ann in lover's flare.

However that may be, her wounded pride
And silent sigh touched Abe; his heart was kind,
He sympathized with innocence and tried
In ways to comfort Ann. He searched to find
And brighten lonely hours for her, to hide
From critics' eyes the wound McNeil designed.

---

* McNeil left New Salem. His long silence caused Ann anxiety, and her parents and friends came to believe him unworthy of her. Ann was glad that Lincoln seemed to understand her situation, like a big brother, and she gladly accepted his companionship as such.[22]

ABE BEFRIENDS ANN
1834

A year dragged by. McNeil* had ceased to write,
So Abe and Ann, as friends, went everywhere
Until it seemed that Ann had not a care.
And with their day's work done, they went at night
To Mentor Graham—lessons to recite,
Or maybe joined in reading something rare
In books or magazines, and Abe would share
His views with Ann in brotherly delight.

Thus passed the time until one day Abe said:
"There are but two weeks more till I go down
To State Assembly halls,† there to be led,
Or else to lead—if I can fit a crown
Of law and justice to my humble head."
"Oh, Abe," Ann smiled, "someday you'll know renown!"

---

* For personal reasons, John *McNamar* had merely assumed the name *McNeil* while Ann had known him in New Salem.[23]

† To Vandalia, the capital.

RUTLEDGE REVERSES
About 1834

Financial loss made Rutledge fortune less.
They left the tavern, moved the family
Out on a farm* nearby, till they could see
Some means to make amends for strain and stress;
The farm gave them a roof and food to bless.
How could they know this move would prove to be
For two of them a grim Gethsemane,
From prairie damps that stalked with ruthlessness!

Death's skeleton shook rattling bones and leered
Its gruesome teeth at all the settlers there,
Well knowing that the marshlands bred and smeared
Foul fevers, chills and typhoid everywhere.
The spring rains loosed these pests that all men feared,
And each claimed victims, leaving blank despair!

---

* The Rutledges moved to McNeil's (McNamar's) farm.[24]

DEATH ENTERS
August 25, 1835

Assembly closed, and Abe—back to survey—
Called on "Miss Ann." They walked a prairie lane,
Discussed his State Assembly work and gain . . .
While prairie fevers followed them. One day
They snatched Ann's breath and took her soul away.*
Abe mourned her—missed her friendly smile—with pain
More keen than does a bird in flight when rain
Of shot makes its companion, hunter's prey.

Abe walked the streets in youthful heartfelt qualm,
And nursed the sick, laid out the dead; thus he
Who bore the loss of his good friend brought calm
To countless others left in misery.
Immortal friendship,† like some holy psalm,
Lives on within the heart eternally!

---

* Ann Rutledge died August 25, 1835; and her father died in 1836.

† Authors differ as to the relationship of Abe to Ann. No proof has been produced that they were anything more than the best of friends. Herndon's statements have not been substantiated.[25]

ANN'S BURIAL
August 26, 1835

With loving care good friends laid Ann away.
Squire Green, who went with Abe, was shocked to see
Upon his cheeks the fever-flush decree.
"Come, Abe, and rest, nor go out to survey,
Or nurse the sick; your fever's high! Come stay
With us." But Abe refused, "Though worn I be,
It 'pears that work's the only cure for me;
My thanks, good friend, but others need today!"

Most homes had someone sick. Abe's strength was gone,
And friends observed his weary progress home.
"Now, Abe, you're sick," Doc Allen said. "At dawn,
Squire Green will come for you. This germ-filled loam
Is bad! But rest and care, with drops anon,
Will make you fit as sweetened honeycomb."

GRIEF LOST IN EFFORT
1836-1837

Sometimes a recompense for grief has brought
Great good. Abe's came in recognition due.
Assemblymen saw Abe could pilot through
Each issue that had controversial thought.
Denied the Speakership of House, Abe wrought
So well as "Master Whig" that men there knew
His wisdom visioned ways to best construe
All measures of the State as honor taught.

The awkward, rawboned Abe began to dim;
Instead, his constant growth caused men to see
A master mind, a genius poised in him.
His humor brought congeniality;
His clean, clear reasoning gave mental vim
To drive each issue through with mastery.

THE INTERNAL IMPROVEMENTS BILL
1836-1837

No Legislative session worked for more,
Historically, than did the Tenth.* The state,
In need of transportation, brought debate
On building railways, roads, how to explore
The waterways to open traffic's door.
They planned two trunk railways: one to run straight
From north to south, and one to operate
Across, while spurs led from a central core.

Two hundred thousand[27] they proposed to spend
In counties not traversed by railway line,
To build good roads so farmers could attend
The markets, selling grain, their sheep and swine.
This lured more pioneers whose aims defend
The glory of his own figtree and vine.

---

* It was in this session of the Assembly that Lincoln first expressed his ideas on slavery, and in which he aided materially in the development of the "Long Nine," which later moved the state capital from Vandalia to Springfield.[26]

Both: Univ. of Ill. Library.

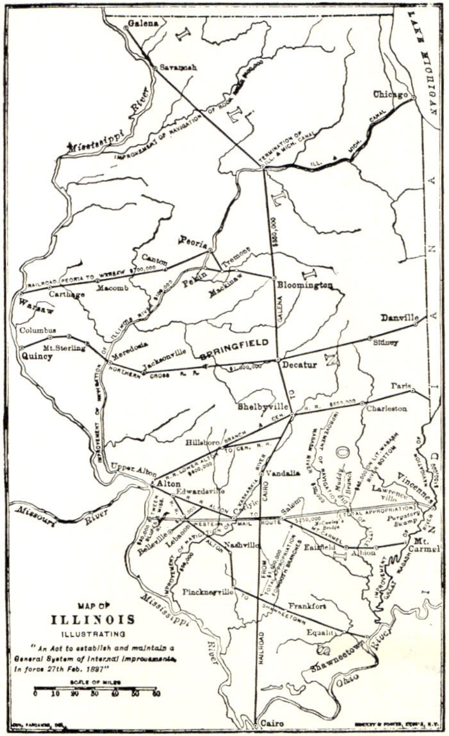

COTILLION PARTY.

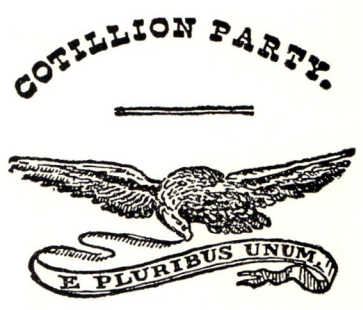

E PLURIBUS UNUM.

The pleasure of your Company is respectfully solicited at a Cotillion Party, to be given at the "American House," on to=morrow evening at 7 o'clock, P. M.

December 16th, 1839

M. M. RIDGELY,	S. F. SPEED,
J. A. M'CLERNAND,	J. SHIELDS,
R. ALLEN,	E. D. TAYLOR,
M. H. WASH,	E. H. MERRYMAN,
C. W. TODD,	N. E. WHITESIDE,
B. A. DOUGLASS,	M. EASTHAM,
W. S. PRENTICE,	J. R. DILLER,
N. W. EDWARDS,	A. LINCOLN,
	Managers.

FACSIMILE OF AN INVITATION TO A SPRINGFIELD COTILLION PARTY OF WHICH A. LINCOLN WAS ONE OF THE MANAGERS.

Left: Map showing canals, river navigation, railroads, and highway improvements authorized by State legislation of 1837, passed at Vandalia with Lincoln's help. *Right*: A survey of Lincoln's social standing in Springfield as shown by his listing among the Cotillion managers in December, 1839.

THE LONG NINE

The talk began in eighteen thirty-three
To move the capital to some place near
The central part of state, for it was clear
The north and central parts had grown to be
More dense in population. All could see
The need for change, yet powwows held each year
By bidding towns* in combat, felt much fear
To lose, and therefore, "tabled" annually.

In eighteen thirty-seven there was passed,
By "Lincoln's skill" and the "Long Nine,"† the vote
That gave to Springfield the most honored place
As capital of state. They stood enmassed
Throughout their time on many things of note,
And legend still proclaims their fame and grace.

---

* Among the towns competing for the capital of Illinois were Peoria, Jacksonville, Alton, Decatur, Vandalia and Springfield.

† The "Long Nine" was composed of men whose average height was six feet or more. Lincoln was usually their leader. The others were: Dan Stone, William F. Elkins, John Dawson, R. L. Wilson, Andrew McCormick, Ninian Edwards of the House, and Job Fletcher and Archer Herndon of the Senate.[28]

LINCOLN MOVES TO SPRINGFIELD
April, 1837

With Springfield capital, it lured, apace,
Young Abe to change his residence.[*] The need
Of room and bed sent him to meet Josh Speed.[†]
Each liked the other's attitude and face,
And Speed then asked, "Well, why not share my place?
It's up above my store. If you're agreed,
I'll take you in. We'll go elsewhere to feed."
A lifelong friendship born, soon waxed in grace.

All day Abe practiced Law. His cases, few
At first, expanded gradually. At night
He went with Josh or Stuart[§] as a new
Adherent to the younger set. Bedight
With wit and drollery, he quickly grew
In favor, filling all with much delight.

---

[*] April 15, 1837.
[†] Joshua Fry Speed kept a furniture store.
[§] John T. Stuart was Lincoln's law partner.

STUART AND LINCOLN, LAWYERS
April, 1837

With law examinations passed,[*] Abe's star
Shone brightly with his partner Stuart where,
In Springfield, both were known and welcomed. There,
As time ran by, fame's cloak was spread afar.
Each colleague felt a valid cause to spar
As representative of state. The pair
Were known as men of wisdom who would dare
To wage their cause for justice at the bar.

The Lincoln arguments were strong, and spun
In documented proof with truth as might.
His store of legal knowledge, wit and fun
Impressed his listeners and would unite
The judging jurymen, and thus, Abe won
By small distinctions, as men now will cite.

---

[*] Lincoln had passed his bar examination, September 9, 1836 and on March 1, 1837 had been formally admitted to the bar.[29]

SPRINGFIELD, CAPITAL OF ILLINOIS
1839

Abe's Springfield* was a midwest village where
Assemblymen met now on tree-filled ground
Midst prairie scenes. The houses sprawled around
In all directions from the village square.
The chickens, pigs and cows all made aware
That something *new* had come, with startling sound
Of sudden cackles, squeals and moos, soon found
Escape through muddy streets with outraged air.

Although the town was not three thousand yet,
Its hospitality was warm and gay.
It boasted of its younger social set
That welcomed legislators when they play.
These merry times none likely would forget,
As Springfield's youth pursued true festive sway.

---

* Governor Thomas Carlin had, on July 4, 1839, proclaimed Springfield as the new capital of Illinois. It had a population of about 2,500. Some lived in palatial homes and others in log cabins, but their stock ran loose through the streets.[30]

SPRINGFIELD'S SOCIAL LIFE

When Springfield won the capital of state
It sought to measure up in social rites.
Its hostesses assembled guests for nights
Of gaiety and song. There was no wait;
A big cotillion, first upon the slate,
Began the festivals for neophytes
Well sponsored by the local socialites,
Among whom Lincoln's name had come to rate.*

Those early days are still recalled for teas,
For picnics, skating, sports and dinners too.
They much enjoyed square dances, spelling bees,
And organ-singing groups—songs old and new;
And always folks would meet at obsequies.
But gay or sad, such days we still review.

---

* Authors have said that when Lincoln came to Springfield he had no social position, which is a mistake. He knew the best of families there, among whom were Speed, the Stuarts, the Edwardses, and the Logans. *See p. 51a, this volume, facsimile of Cotillion Invitation.*

REWARDS OF EFFORT
1839-1841

Reward of toil is not what man is paid
In paltry gold, but what toil makes of him
In doing it. Abe's clear insight and vim
Were recognized, yet by opponents stayed
Until his diction clarified and weighed
His principles, though some they thought were whim.
Abe's genial humor flashed its golden rim
To frame the chain of logic he assayed.

Sometimes Abe toiled in study all the night,[31]
But from this grew a statesmanship to mold
The minds of men by power of truth that right
Is strength, a godly heritage to hold
For his young State. His mind became a light
For lesser men who measure gains by gold.

ELECTORAL COLLEGE CANDIDATE
1838-1840

Abe polled the highest vote in 'thirty-eight
And 'forty earned by anyone who ran
For legislative office. In the van
As leader of the Whigs, it was his fate
For men to boost him up to higher state.*
Thus, at the Whig Convention there began
And carried on for sixteen years, the plan
To build Abe's prestige to its highest rate.[32]

These vibrant years were full for Abe. With Law,
Judicial Circuit, Representative,
And speaking tours for President, folks saw
Him burdened, yet his wish to gladly give
The best he knew, left records free of flaw
That taught: Growth comes in learning how to live.

---

* To make him a member of the Electoral College, whose privilege it is to vote in the President and Vice-President of the United States. *See Addendum Note* [32].

ON THE CIRCUIT
1839-1859

Perhaps no part of Lincoln's legal life
Gave him more joy than did his early days
When on the Circuit[33] rounds he rode by chaise
Or horse through muddy roads to settle strife.
The county seats where courts were held were rife
With news that all discussed. And girls in stays
And hoops and men in silk cravats, through maze
Of laughter, danced to fiddle, harp, and fife.

Court days were gala times when farmers took
Their produce into town to trade for lace
Or silk, or rice or tea, perhaps a book!
Some nights they talked or asked Abe to their place
To spend the hours, while legal minds would look
Him up to seek opinions on some case.

CIRCUIT COURTS
1839

The cases tried in every circuit court*
Were those of thieving, libel, loss, assault,
The ownership of hogs, or whose the fault
For livestock damages or such ill sport;
Divorce, and slander based on false report.
Sometimes a shocking murder trial would vault
The winning lawyer into fame, exalt
His legal stature through his licit forte.

At times, the lawyers hired to try a case
Would number three or four, and often they
Would travel cavalcade with comrade grace,
En route through prairie roads that marked their way.
Companionship was sweet, with storms to face
Or hours that dragged throughout a sunny day.

---

* These courts lasted usually three days to a week. Lawyer Lincoln's income per year was $1,200 to $1,500 (as compared to the judge's annual salary of $750 and the governor's $1,200), but this was often paid in groceries, vegetables or livestock.[34]
See map of 8th Judicial Circuit, p. 32a, this volume.

LINCOLN MEETS MARY TODD
1839

All Springfield knew of Lincoln long before
He came as resident to practice law.
His popularity was soon to draw
His name to dine and grace the dancing floor.
One night he met Miss Todd.* "I could adore
A girl like her," he may have thought with awe,
For he was shy of girls, yet when he saw
Her eyes and grace, his courage rose to soar.

"Miss Todd, I want to dance with you worst way,"
He said. She gave consent with roguish smile.
And as they danced, the more he tried to stay
His leaping heart, the more she would beguile
His thought until his feet would tend to stray.
She gasped, "He did dance *worst way* all the while!"

---

* Mary Todd came from Lexington, Kentucky. She was the sister of Mrs. Ninian Edwards and lived in their home. Ninian Edwards was Mary's guardian. She was an attractive, lively girl.

THE ONE REALITY

Since both were known in Springfield's younger set,
Abe saw her often, liked her social grace.
She liked his intellect and honest face.
Sometimes he took her home; they then would net
An hour of gain from Shakespeare's plays. She let
Him read the lines, or maybe each would trace
Some character through act and scenes apace.
These treasured hours they neither could forget.

The weeks soon passed and each had come to know
That their relationship was more than friends.
Each felt, within, the warmth of subtle ray
That soon began to burn and brighter glow ...
Love's dawn—a mystery that never ends!
For ever thus have young hearts felt love's sway.

OBJECTIONS

The Lincoln courtship had been carried on
For months when arrogance and rank began
To greet him with a chilly air, to ban
His frequent visits.* With his welcome gone,
His vanity was stabbed. No myrmidon,
Brave Mary disregarded kindred clan
When they advised, a rich and noble man
Should be her choice to earn their benison.

But Mary's love was deep, sincere, and wide.
Her joy was in Abe's independence, shown
In gracious thought, and in his mental stride.
She said, "No, I shall wed for love. My own
Abe Lincoln is the one to safely guide
My heart's desire. No other shall dethrone!"

---

* Authors differ as to the cause of the broken engagement of Lincoln and Mary, but since the Edwardses were aristocrats they likely thought that Mary could make a more advantageous marriage. For fear that his further attentions might be an injustice to her, Lincoln decided to release her.[35]

INTROSPECTION

Abe Lincoln felt the pain—the fire of love
That adverse winds had fanned to fervid glow.
Its loss would deal Abe's life a drastic blow.
"But is she mine?" he asked. "No force above
Can move my heart till sure. Affection's glove
Must fit the heart it lures. Each must bestow
Much discipline to understand and know
The other's wish, as does each turtledove.

All this I feel and wish to do, but she—
She comes of noble blood while I am born
A commoner—[36] Would fondness mark our years?
Or would they soon wear down to misery?*
Dear God, would that I knew! Send light of morn
That I may ban my hopes and spare her tears!"

---

* Lincoln loved Mary but doubted his ability to support a wife who was a pampered aristocrat. Lincoln broke the engagement.

"THE FATAL FIRST OF JAN'Y"[*]
1841

All looked with favor on this charming pair,
With Mary's boasted lineage descent
And Lincoln's simple, modest mien, well blent
With growing confidence and friendly air.
Yet few could understand or be aware
That clash of blood had formed a discontent
Which left two youthful lovers' dreams well rent,
That hopeless hearts in agony reigned there.

On New Year's Day the word spread like wild fire
That lovers' quarrel sent each on his way.
Some said she jilted Abe in female ire,
And that he grieved and pined the livelong day.
But some thought pride in blood had built the pyre
To sacrifice their love, though none dared say.

---

[*] Lincoln's own words.[37]

LOGAN AND LINCOLN
April, 1841-December, 1844

The Stuart, Lincoln partners were both deep
In politics, and neither one could spare
The hours for office work. Each was aware
The partnership must be dissolved. A heap
Of work engaged Judge Logan's desk.* To keep
It all, the Judge sought Lincoln's aid to share
In it as partner. Lincoln joined, and there
Found legal knowledge that his need could reap.

For here with Logan, Lincoln learned to hold
A jury . . . how to plead and how to bring,
Through careful preparation of each case,
A clarity of meaning . . . knack to mold
The juror's thoughts throughout the questioning.
This careful practice brought him fame and grace.

---

* Stephen T. Logan was known as an excellent legal technician. He had been Judge of the First Judicial Circuit and was a member of the State Assembly from 1842-1848. He had been on the bench in Lincoln's first case and recalled "the quality and promise of Lincoln's talents. . ." Thomas says, "The Lincoln-Logan partnership developed into one of the leading firms of the state. . ."[38]

THE ESTRANGEMENT
1841

The lonely lovers tried in vain to find
Some small relief from heartache's keen despair
By seeking others with whom they could share
The dragging time. Young Webb* made plans designed
To win Miss Todd. They chatted, danced and dined.
Then Stephen Douglas wooed with cultured air,
While Lincoln took Miss Edwards† here and there.
But neither felt a love with force to bind.

And so for months pride held its baneful ground;
Some said that Abe avoided meeting her,
But Lincoln's remedy for ills was found
In *work,* and none was ever kindlier
Than that in which the Circuit Courts abound—
There, thrived democracy without a blur.

---

* Edwin B. Webb was a young widower with two children, and Stephen A. Douglas enjoyed Mary's company. But Mary still loved Lincoln.

† Lincoln took Matilda Edwards and Sarah Rickard out now and then, and corresponded with Mary Owens.

IRISH IRE
1842

A panic* wrought hard times through many years,
While Shields was acting Auditor of State
Demanding gold and silver as the rate
Of fair exchange. Then Satire's vicious sneers
Against his acts began in letter-jeers,†
And Lincoln authored one. At later date
Young Mary tried her hand. These roused Shields' hate,
And he sought Abe to squash these lethal smears.
Abe Lincoln's chivalry assumed the blame
For both the letters that had caused Shields' ire.
Shields challenged Lincoln to a duel. Name
And honor were at stake; Abe knew hate's pyre
Must burn, and so accepted. Fears aflame,
Abe's friends then stopped the fight, and quenched the fire.[39]

---

* The panic of 1837.

† Because Auditor James Shields was a Democrat, the Whig newspaper, *Sangamo Journal,* ran a series known as "the 'Rebecca' letters" ridiculing Shields in a form of satire then in vogue. These letters irritated Shields and he demanded a duel.

LOVE IS ETERNAL*
November 4, 1842

When Mary learned that Lincoln's chivalry
Had risked a duel just to shield her name,
Her warm heart thrilled with joy's wild leaping flame.
For knowing Abe still loved her set her free
To hope for those good times that used to be,
When life had held one precious thought and aim.
Then, Mrs. Francis† tried a little game
By asking Abe to join a friend at tea.

When Abe arrived—he saw Miss Todd! No guile
Was meant, nor could be lodged, yet unaware,
Dan Cupid stood and smirked a roguish smile;
His arrow bound two hearts in love's sweet snare
That made "till death do part" a rose-strewn isle,
And Parson Dresser made them *one*§ by prayer.

---

* Lincoln had these words engraved in Mary's wedding ring.

† Mrs. Simeon Francis, wife of the *Sangamo Journal* editor, brought them together.[40]

§ Abraham Lincoln and Mary Todd were married November 4, 1842.

THE HONEYMOON

The news of Todd's and Lincoln's marriage flew
About and over town and countryside;
Surprise for some, but all seemed satisfied
That love would bind them till earth-life was through.
Then Abe procured a room and board for two
At old Globe Tavern, where they would reside
Until such time as income would provide
A house with trees and flowers, a yard and view.

Their months of sore estrangement having passed,
The love that had been quelled, now gathered power
Within their hearts, their eyes, their lips and words—
Like bubbling springs. They found content at last,
And felt more joy and confidence each hour,
Which thrilled them like the caroling of birds.

THE STORK'S VISIT
August 1, 1843

"The Lincolns have a baby!"* neighbors said—
"They named it Robert Todd for Mary's dad.†
An' Lincoln—he's plum foolish 'bout th' lad
An' talks to it when he comes near its bed.
Its eyes are gray, got brown hair on its head,
An'—how that child can cry! He gets so mad
He yells an' yells! The Globe folks will be glad
When Lincolns move—no sleep without a dread!"

And Mary found the Globe a noisy place,
Too noisy for her babe—feet stamped the stair,
With clang of servant's bell! She wanted space—
And so they soon moved out to Fourth Street where
They had a three-room house that held no trace
Of tavern smoke, and quietness was there.§

---

* Mary said later, "My darling husband was bending over me, with such love and tenderness . . ." when the child was born.[41]

† The Lincoln baby was a great event to Mary's widower father. Within a few weeks, he came to see his namesake and perhaps to inspect his son-in-law. He went home well pleased.

§ They lived in this little frame cottage only during the winter of 1843-1844. It was located at 214 South Fourth Street. [42]

LINCOLN BUYS A HOME
1844

Though from six years' law practice Abe had paid
Store debt,* and loaned his father sums, one year
In Logan's partnership had put his fear
To rout. All legal work they had essayed
Had grown; his Circuit cases all had made
Good pay increase. He now felt free to steer
His hopes to meet a need for those held dear:
A home with lawn and trees and flowering glade.

Since Parson Dresser had just such a place
On Eighth and Jackson, built of seasoned board,
Abe said, "My darling, you would surely grace
That house." Then thoughtfully, "I'll count my hoard;
If you would like, I'll buy!" He watched her face—
Saw questioning, "Yes, now, I can afford."[43]

---

* The debt which Lincoln had assumed when his New Salem store partner Berry died. For Lincoln's annual income during these years, *see footnote on p. 61, this volume.*

EDWARD BAKER LINCOLN
March 10, 1846

Before three years there came a second son
To bless their home—a lovely child, folks say,
Named Edward, for Abe's colleague.* Every day
He grew and thrived, good natured little one.
With Abe's day work complete and supper done,
They all sat by the fire. Such time for play
Made Abe lighthearted, Edward zestful, gay;
"Come, Eddie Boy," Abe said, "we'll have some fun!"

Abe took him up and rocked him to and fro,
He tossed him in and out and up and down
Till Eddie's laughter filled the air, then— slow
And slower— did they rock till Shut-eye-town
Was reached, and love's soft crooning bade Ed go
To sleep, while angels' watchful silence crown.

---

* Edward Dickinson Baker.

LINCOLN

SERVES

THE PEOPLE AND A CAUSE

LINCOLN RUNS FOR CONGRESS
1846

Through Whig political maneuverings*
Abe Lincoln reached the goal as candidate
For Congress. Peter Cartwright, famed as great
Evangelist, opposed Abe's aim. The wings
Of hope in Abe still sailed where triumph clings,
Yet he recalled a former race for State
Assembly Cartwright seized.† "But now—this gate,"
Abe thought, "may stand ajar—I'll pull the strings."

Perhaps no one revivalist was known
Who challenged men to turn to what is best,
As Cartwright did. In politics, not so!
He said Abe was an atheist§ . . . enthrone
Abe in an office would be evil's jest.
But Lincoln's hopes lured him with steady glow.

---

* By "maneuverings" we refer to the agreement between John J. Hardin, Edward D. Baker and Lincoln as to the rotation of the Whig candidacy for Congress between the three of them.

† In 1832 Peter Cartwright and Lincoln had run for the State Assembly, and Peter Cartwright had won.

§ For Lincoln's reply to Cartwright's unfounded charges of infidelity, *see Addendum Note 44.*

MRS. SPRIGG'S BOARDINGHOUSE
1847

Elected, Lincoln with his family
Took rooms in Washington,* quite near the lawn
That held the Capitol. At morning's dawn
They saw it framed beneath one big park tree
In grand outline—rich view for memory.
But boardinghouses have their rules close-drawn
And Mary, with her romping sons, was gone
Within four months, so they could live more free.

While at the boardinghouse some careworn guest
No doubt sensed much relief, all held respect
For Abe and filled his loneliness with jest
Or tale. Each man would carefully select
Some story that he then would tell with zest;
But their art paled compared with Abe's effect.

---

* At Mrs. Sprigg's Boardinghouse, where many other Senators and Congressmen were rooming.[45]

THE SPOT RESOLUTION
December 22, 1847

Now James K. Polk, as shown in history,[*]
Was pledged by partisans who swore to dare
And seize a neighbor's land. Though no affair
So foul or more unjust could ever be,
Pro-slave men urged it as necessity,
While Polk claimed "self-defense." Abe asked, "Just where
Did war with Mexico begin?" aware
The spot Polk named was Mexico, per se.[†]

All Congress sat in silent shock! Some tried
To justify Polk's scheme by showing gain
In land, which Whigs well knew they meant to use
For slave extensions. With Whig aims denied,
As pro-slave Congress knew, it seemed most vain
To struggle for their rights against such ruse.

---

[*] James K. Polk was an Expansionist.

[†] The first blood was spilled April 23, 1846 at Fort Brown on Mexican soil. The war lasted only two years, but Polk acquired to the United States not only Texas, but New Mexico, Arizona and California. *See Addendum Note 46.*

GROWING CONFLICT

All felt a growing conflict in the air:
The war with Mexico—though launched with plea
Of self-defense—was wrought by trickery,*
As all men knew; for some with little care
Had closed their eyes to methods used for share
In gain. So David Wilmot's loyalty
Declared men's rights are sacred and must be
Upheld by justice, honor, faith and prayer.

Yet his Proviso,† Congress soon denied
By Democratic strength. Then, came Abe's bill
To liberate Columbia's drove of slaves§
Kept chained in pens. But though he worked as guide,
It failed to come to vote— Abe urged it still,
Held freemen's rights as sacred to their graves!

---

* General U. S. Grant said: "We were sent to provoke a fight, but it was essential that Mexico should commence it. It was very doubtful whether Congress would declare war;" unless in self-defense. Mexico was a poor, weak neighbor. She had a small army and was not prepared for war. *See Addendum Note 47.*

† Wilmot's Proviso, added to an appropriation bill, would have prohibited slavery in territory gained from Mexico.

§ Lincoln wrote a bill to abolish slavery in the District of Columbia, but it did not reach consideration by Congress.[48]

CONDEMNATION

When voters learned that war with Mexico
Had brought the States at least a third more land,
Few were not pleased. The Democrats then planned
To oust Abe, should he try again to go
To Washington as Congressman, a foe
To slavery. They knew his moral stand
Would not consent to sell his soul for *sand*
That might in time become a nation's woe.

Abe's sense of human value clamored strong:
He saw the soil as worth, till Polk's false claim[49]
Had proved the conquest most unfair and wrong—
Their nation on its knees, our guns aflame;
Polk's vicious move would cast, in time, a throng
Of critics' censure on our nation's name.

MARY VISITS LEXINGTON
1848-1849

The Lincoln children had small discipline,
For winsome Mary held a selfish creed:
"Oh, let them have their way!" She failed to heed
Their trespassing on others' rights with din
That brought confusion, and to some, chagrin.
Her father wrote to urge her meet a need
By coming as his guest. This did indeed
Bring joy and peace to lodgers at the inn.[*]

How much the Lincolns felt their loneliness,
Apart, is shown by letters which they penned;
Not one is left but breathes its love caress.
And all the while, Abe seemed to apprehend
Forebodings[†] that were given added stress
In statements proving true love has no end.

---

[*] In the spring of 1848, Mary Lincoln and her two sons went and remained for some time as house guests in her father's home in Lexington, Kentucky.[50]

[†] Lincoln's love for his family was so strong that he worried when they were away from him and his fatherly protection.

LETTERS AND PLAID STOCKINGS
April 16, 1848

The note that Mary sent brought Abe a smile.
"She wants a little pair of new plaid hose,"
Said Abe, while searching shops' display of clothes,
"They're for our 'codger'!"* And he shopped a while
To find a pair, but though he searched the pile
Where Allens' mixed displays of such repose,
Not one was found of proper size. He chose
To try again next day, for length and style.

In his replies, among the things he said[51]
Were that he hoped she hired a helpful maid
To take charge of their boys! He wished her head
Well rid of migraine ache, and longed to aid.
His dream of Bob had worried him. Did Ed
And Bob both like their letters, hers conveyed?

---

* Lincoln's own term of endearment. *See Addendum Note 51.*

SECOND YEAR IN CONGRESS
1848-1849

That summer Abe campaigned throughout the East;
Attended National Convention too,*
Where Whigs put Taylor's nomination through,
With Filmore running mate. Some worries ceased
With Whigs elected in the fall. Like yeast
That leavens dough, Abe's understanding grew
To meet a nation's need. He would subdue
Its wrongs, the evils slavery increased.

When Texas was annexed a slave-state prize
With California free and all aware
That Congress would remain unchanged in mold,
Abe saw slave depots yet confronting eyes
In Washington† and said, "No time to spare,
I'll bring my bill again to break that hold."§

---

* The first time Lincoln had attended a National Convention.

† Lincoln was deeply moved when he still saw flourishing, within a few blocks of the Capitol, a "sort of negro livery-stable" in which "droves of negroes were collected . . . precisely like droves of horses. . ."[52]

§ Lincoln's bill to remove slave depots from the National Capital failed until he became President.

LINCOLN AND HIS CONTEMPORARIES
1848-1849

Each day in Congress with the nation's great
Found Lincoln contemplating leading men.
Observing artifice and power, he then,
By keen comparison, soon learned to rate
His own deficiencies. Nor did he wait,
But eagerly sought aid from books,† and when
At leisure, read each helpful one again
To fix in mind some point to cogitate.

And some contemporaries recognized
His latent power, which still lacked mastery;
Some also noted how Abe ever prized
To talk with learned ones as remedy,
Not letting mental hunger lie disguised
Beneath his friend-sired popularity.

---

* The Thirteenth Congress ranked high in intelligence and ability.[53]

† The Library of Congress recorded 125 books checked out by Lincoln, besides the many that he may have secured elsewhere.

"GONE TAPILA"
1848

A letter fresh from Lexington* had brought
Good news. Bob, four, was lively as could be
And Eddie, just past two, tried constantly
To talk. His growing intellect had sought
His father, 'cross the park. His mother taught
And showed him *Capitol* so when this wee
Lad missed his father most, his mind would see
The *"tap-i-la"* in his "Where's father?" thought.

Thus Mrs. Lincoln sent this anecdote
When they were visiting in Lexington:
"Dear Eddy thinks his father's *gone*," she wrote,
"*'Gone tapila'*."[54] Abe was assured this one
Had not forgotten† him. He loved to quote,
"*'Gone tapila'*—My precious little son!"

---

* Lexington, Kentucky. Lincoln's answer was dated "April 16, 1848—".

† Lincoln had a fear that his young sons might forget him in being separated from him for several months. Mary's letter reassured him that they had missed him and talked of him. *See Addendum Note 54.*

LINCOLN'S SOCIAL STANDING
Congress, 1848

Despite Abe's frontier dialect and drawl,
Men saw his giant intellect as might
To reckon with, that prophesied a height
Beyond most minds. He earned respect of all
By speeches that he gave in Congress' hall.
He guarded manners, sat with erudite
At Webster's breakfast,* few were more polite.
And he advised at Seward's, Wilmot's call.†

When Preston, Toombs and Stevens had begun
To form a Taylor Club, they sent Abe where
Campaign had need.§ In Tremont Temple, one,
A *Levi Lincoln*,[55] governor up there,
Asked Abe to dinner. When the meal was done
They traced through ancestors a kinship rare.

---

* Webster's breakfast was the social event of that session. Only the elite were there.

† Lincoln was popular as a member of Congressional committees.

§ Lincoln campaigned around Washington, through New England, and in Illinois.

DEATH OF JOHN QUINCY ADAMS
1848

Earth's workday closed for one great patriot
In Congress, February twenty-three.
As Adams rose to speak, dire tragedy
Stepped in to interfere, by fatal clot.
Death seized the aging Adams, on the spot.
His speaking faltered, breath came short . . . and he
Sank helpless to his chair! Unconsciously
Peace came—his struggling nation was forgot!*

When some great moral issue was at stake,
There stood John Quincy Adams staunch and true;
Defiant, firm, till enemies would quake.
Thus Adams-Lincoln admiration grew.†
And Congress named, with Lincoln, men to make
Some honor plans befitting this man's due.

---

* The 84-year-old former President died of a stroke at his desk in the Congressional hall during a session in 1848.

† Lincoln and Adams were in agreement politically, and each held a deep admiration for the other, which had ripened into a warm friendship.

WHEN CONGRESS CLOSED
1849

When Congress heard its last long speech and mills
Of law had ceased, Abe realized his dream—
To try a case within the Court Supreme.*
Then, too, a patent granted him† brought thrills,
A means to hoist boats over sandbar hills.
When Abe entrained for home,§ he visioned gleam
Of prairie lands with winding, rippling stream
Where spring's fresh winds danced golden daffodils.
He pictured all once more—his Illinois!
As train and boat sped west through countryside,
His mind formed future plans nought could destroy:
His firm resolve to practice law and ride
The Circuit once again, and know the joy
Of humble folk—his folk—there to abide.

---

* Lincoln lost his case in the United States Supreme Court, and failed to get his desired appointment to the Land Office.

† Lincoln was granted patent rights, May 22, 1849, on "a new and improved manner of combining adjustable buoyant chambers with steam boats or other vessels."[56]

§ Lincoln returned by train and boat. The big railroad period was soon to come, but had not yet arrived.

HAD LINCOLN FAILED?
1847-1851

When man has stood alone for right, success
Will crown his work in time, as all must see.
Though some were sure Abe failed them utterly,
Such judgment came from pure shortsightedness,
Or counterparties seeking to oppress.
Abe's conscience would not stoop to travesty,[*]
As later was revealed by history.
Abe Lincoln stood for right without redress.

And when, at home, death's angel unaware
Had claimed his little son and father, too,[†]
Such grief plus critics' thrusts, no man could bear
Alone. Abe sought God's gracious guidance through
The lonely weeks, and thus by work and prayer
There came to him a faith and trust anew.

---

[*] Although Lincoln regarded the Mexican War as unjust, he voted supplies for our men in the war, as is shown by Congressional records.

[†] Lincoln's four-year-old son, Eddie, died February 1, 1850; his father, Tom Lincoln, died January 17, 1851.

BACK ON THE CIRCUIT
1840-1858

Now while the wrangling states knew strife and hate,
And men in schooners traveled west for gold,*
Abe Lincoln drove through mud and dust to mold
Men's minds, explaining laws that compensate.
These were his years of greatest growth. Innate
Desire to learn and rise, from uncontrolled
To perfect English speech, had made him bold
To gain more skill and power to animate.

Abe read his Bible, Shakespeare, ancient lore;
Cleared statutes, read his Blackstone, Equity;
He studied *men,* and read the papers more
For national events and summary.
Abe, thus, made gains in culture that could soar
Beyond the heights which common man may see.

---

* Gold was discovered in California in 1848.

CIRCUIT REVERIES
1850

The springtime sun poured gold upon the trees,
It etched illumined dapples on the grass.
As Lincoln rode he heard the bluejay's sass,
The dove's soft coo, and felt a gentle breeze
Upon his cheek; yet mind could sense no ease.
He saw his youth, as in a mirrored glass,
And noted every rise and fall—a mass
Of treasured dreams that youth had sought to seize.

Each conquest gnawed the fiber of his soul
Till, like a house of blocks, his dream world fell
For him to build into more perfect whole.
He saw life's road, and mused: "No yawning hell
Of failure's fears shall ever block my goal,
I shall arrive! *Faith* rings a victor's bell!"*

---

* Lincoln was determined to succeed in whatever he attempted to do. He was constantly comparing his real with his ideal, his past with his present, and thereby he made a rapid growth.

LINCOLN'S CHARACTER GROWTH
1849-1852

In manner simple, yet Abe's thoughts would climb;
Though humble, self-reliance held him true
And trained his mind to analytic view.
Though practical, his thinking was sublime—
Was undemonstrative, yet deep; at prime,
Unfathomed tenderness and pity grew.
Abe was conservative, much caution knew;
Self-made, he flourished like the prairie thyme.

He had an open friendly way, yet *will*
Maintained reticence destined to repel
Familiarity—but hold men, still.
His magnetism would draw men to tell
Their thoughts in confidence;[57] though versatile,
He was closemouthed and silent as a shell.

MOULTRIE COUNTY CIRCUIT COURT
1852

The Moultrie Courthouse, built of brick, was new;
It graced the county seat in Sullivan.*
Since Robert Crowder's interests all ran
Toward right and justice, this he did pursue,
Attending court to hear all cases through.†
But when at home, experience to scan,
He sat and chuckled as he said, "That man—
That Lincoln lawyer—sure knows what to do!

He has a lot of wit, is full of fun,
And knows just how to tell a joke to win
A point, or loose the tension of each one—
Like when he told about King Nero's sin
And how he set old Rome on fire, and none
Could put it out ... while he sat fid-dl-in!"

---

* Moultrie became a county in Illinois, January 1, 1843. The Crowders were pioneers and had lived in Marrowbone Township (so called from a small creek by that name) since 1837, when Moultrie was still a part of Shelby and Macon counties.

† Because the Eighth Judicial Circuit legal work became too heavy in 1853, owing to increase in population, Moultrie County was transferred to another Circuit. But *see map of 8th Judicial Circuit, p. 32a, this volume.*

"UNCLE BOBBY"
1852

Now Robert Crowder had eight sons; one, Jim,
A boy of ten with mind both strong and keen,
Had heard his Pappy's tales and longed to glean
Such virtue as Abe Lincoln had—the vim
Of story art! Jim begged to ride with him
To court. His Pappy said: "Well, wash up clean,
And we'll be off at dawn—we'll ride old Queen,
A safe old nag—just comb your hair right trim."

They rode one horse; Jim felt his Pappy's arm
Around him all the way, an hour or so,
Before they reached the fenced-in courthouse yard.*
"Well, James, we're safely here and met no harm.
I'll empty pipe, and brush our clothes of snow,
And tie the mare; the marshal here will guard."

---

* *Inventory of Moultrie County Archives:* "The first Courthouse was brick, 38 x 38, two story and the entire second floor was the courtroom. It was built in 1847."

"MY SON, JAMES"
1852

"Come, Jim, the little courtroom will be filled."
They climbed the long, steep stairs and Jim could see
A tall man breaking bark against his knee
To feed a fire that belched blue smoke and spilled
Rich odors to be twirled as north winds willed.
The tall man paused and chuckled pleasantly:
"Well, howdy, howdy, Uncle Bob! Now, we
Are glad you've come! And— who's this boy so chilled?"

"Oh, Mr. Lincoln, this is my son, James."[*]
Abe put his hand upon Jim's head: "My son,
There's lots of room for good boys on this earth
But none at all for bad, who cheat at games!
That's why we have these courts, to help men shun
The evil ways and stand for right and worth."

---

[*] James was perhaps at his most impressionable age. The influence of that day with Lincoln stimulated a desire in him to become such a speaker as Lincoln was. In later years, James did become not only a minister and an evangelist, but was regarded by his contemporaries as "one of the best after-dinner speakers in Illinois."

FAMILY TIES
1849

With court at Charleston,* Lincoln tried to see
His father and "the folks;" or sometimes they
Would sit to hear a case and spend the day
With him—each sought Abe's generosity.[59]
Not since Tom took malaria had he
Been well. John Johnston was not apt to weigh
And share responsibilities. Dismay
Faced Tom, but Abe gave succor tenderly.

Tom owned one hundred acres that were paid
In part. He worked when well enough, though fears
Of loss were felt. Abe saw and gave him aid.
This eased Tom's life through his remaining years;
And in those days, no doubt, Tom often prayed
For Abe, his loyal son, with grateful tears.

---

* Charleston, county seat of Coles County, was on the Circuit. Lincoln was sometimes called in to try a case with a Charleston lawyer. Lincoln's parents had lived nearby in Coles County since 1831. Though we doubtless do not have a record of all of his visits, we do know that in "1849, May, Lincoln visited his father, who was ill."[58]

LINCOLN AND THE LAW
1859

Clay's Compromise in eighteen fifty brought
A lull between the states, yet imminent
In all their views, each tried to orient
Its principles; while Lincoln yearly fought
To build a legal practice, which he sought
Through increased Circuit cases. There, he lent
To every case he tried, strong argument
So clear his adversary's views were naught.

The Lincoln friendliness made him a guest
In homes where people sensed their views akin;
Abe practiced clarity of speech,* to wrest
All ambiguities and thereby win
His hearer's mind. For years this was his quest,
And thus he grew by constant discipline.

---

* Lincoln was a meticulous thinker. He was never satisfied with a thought until he had bounded it on the east, west, north and south so that he could express it in its clearest and simplest meaning.

RELAXATION

His analytic mind prized each detail
Of law, or friend, or meadow greenery.
Abe rode for miles between the courts, could see
The smallest beauty there on hill or dale
Where lurked the fox or more elusive quail,
Could hear the robin's song, the buzzing bee,
Which eased his mind from legal thought's decree
And rested and relaxed him on the trail.

But when at last the Circuit Courts were through
And Abe's old horse turned home—a place most dear,*
He heard his small sons calling, "I love you!"
With Mary in the door, as horse came near.
All worries ceased as arms enclasped—Abe knew
His cup was filled with lasting joy and cheer.

---

* No matter how weary Lincoln was, after weeks of court grind and travel, he anticipated his homecomings with much the same thrill as a small boy anticipates Santa Claus. Home with loved ones was a picture of heaven itself to him.

"OF SUCH IS THE KINGDOM OF HEAVEN"
February 1, 1850

Small Eddie had been ill for weeks; his care
Taxed Mary's strength, so Lincoln soothed his cry
By holding him in arms to pacify,
Or maybe, rock him in some squeaky chair.
One day, as they both watched, Abe saw the stare
Of anxious fear in Mary's tear-dimmed eye,
And as they sat beside him hours sped by,
While each in wordless silence knew despair!

Both felt the gnawing pain, the mystery
Of death, as pallor blanched the baby's face
And—breathing ceased![60] A sunbeam tenderly
Caressed his lips and danced through window lace.
His four short years had left a melody
Engraved upon love-records to retrace.*

---

* On Eddie Lincoln's tombstone were these words: "Of such is the kingdom of Heaven." After Lincoln's death Eddie's coffin was placed in the Lincoln Monument with his family.

THE CHRISTMAS GIFT
December 21, 1850

The poignant pain of Eddie's death was keen,
And many unsolved questions came to mind:
The thought of life beyond and here; to find
Connections safe and sure that led between!
Their Christian friends explained the life unseen
Which gave new hope and faith that would unblind
Their eyes to let them see all life designed
Through love. Yet loneliness is hard to wean.

December twenty-first there came a gift,
A healing Christmas gift—a newborn son.
They named him William Wallace.* Such a lift
As few had known came with this paragon!
An even-tempered, cherub-child ... adrift ...
From heaven's shore, sought anchorage—and won!

---

* Named for Mary Lincoln's brother-in-law, Dr. William Smith Wallace.

DEATH OF TOM LINCOLN
January 17, 1851

Death's message came. Abe read in tears. Long planned
Were five court cases, none he could delay!
The pending Senate bill he could not stay,
Nor I. C. Railroad's case, with its demand
That he must win! Abe understood their stand,[*]
Yet visualized his father, with dismay,
Reposed for burial that winter day—
The kindly face, the hard-worked horny hand.

Tom's years had brought no idle hours;[†] his hoe,
His axe and plow had borne his loved ones through
With food and clothes, had banished frontier woe.
His story-telling, woodcraft skill, all knew
Excelled. His willing heart served friend and foe.
Abe treasured all these traits, in sad review.

---

[*] "You never find Lincoln's activities held up by his inner sufferings."[61]

[†] Tom Lincoln had a drive for work, which he passed on to Abraham.[62]

STUMBLING BLOCKS

Tom's gifts, with faith in God, were coronets
That toil had earned in his community,
And though his lack of schooling—Abe could see—
Had multiplied his struggles and regrets,*
Had set up stumbling blocks of loss and threats,
Hope had endured. Tom worked tenaciously,
Despite poor health and lack of earning fee;
He lived life well—died free from any debts.

Abe sat alone within his office room
And re-appraised his father's worthy life,
Sat——till the sun was lost in twilight gloom.
His pride enthused in one who had known strife,
Yet struggled on, like heel-crushed bud, to bloom.
"Such men," Abe thought, "will always heed the fife!"†

---

* Tom Lincoln had willing hands, but lacked the education to ease his efforts.[63]

† The fife is a symbol of the militant call to *action*.

LINCOLN'S SACRIFICE
January 17, 1851

And so they buried Tom without his son.*
But when Abe's legal duties were all through
He walked the prairies all alone in new,
Crisp snow. He felt his *duty* had been done
At sacrifice of love. No man can shun
When duty calls, though sorrow may pursue.
Each man must choose and weigh what he should do—
Must ask, "Shall *many* sacrifice, or *one*?"

The cases had been set, men notified
To come from near and far, through winter's gust;
The Senate bill† faced those who would deride
Its worth, and others trailed the icy crust
To hear and aid. Abe wiped his eyes and sighed:
"Mine was the price one pays for being just!"

---

* "1851, May, Lincoln visited his stepmother following the death of his father in January."[64]

†The Illinois Central Railroad had retained Lincoln sometime before January 11, 1851 to represent it in an urgent court case then pending, and to use his influence to secure a needed legislative franchise. *See Addendum Note 65.*

THE MISSOURI COMPROMISE
1820

Louisiana Territory, bought
By Jefferson from France, had come in free.
A part, known as Missouri, came to be
Well occupied by men with slaves they brought
Along. Clay knew all former rulings wrought,
Yet asked Missouri's entrance on its plea
That it become a State with slavery.
Refused, a further compromise was sought.*

Then Thomas, Senator from Illinois,†
Proposed no slaves or slave trade could extend
Beyond Missouri's northwest borderline,
And Congress passed Clay's Compromise with joy.
This had kept Congress wrangling without end,
But settlement soothed all as anodyne.

---

* This Clay-Thomas Compromise set aside *the remainder* of the Louisiana Territory north of 36°-30′ as free, *except* Missouri.

† Thomas, though a Northern man, had Southern leanings; his compromise amendment allowed *Missouri* to come into the Union as *a slave state*.[66]

LITTLE TAD LINCOLN
April 4, 1853

On April fourth of eighteen fifty-three,
Another little "codger"* came to stay,
And cheer the Lincoln home; and right away
They named him Thomas in fond memory
Of Lincoln's Dad. There was no remedy
For forms of speech defects† in that far day,
And Lincoln's babe had such—could barely say
His words in garbled sounds, imperfectly.

Abe's heart was touched. He tried to help his son,
This boy so small—Abe called him, "Little Tad!"*
And made much effort to improve his speech.
They thus became great pals. When work was done
And Lincoln came at night he heard, "Da-Dad!"
This tiny boy then tugged and cried, "T-teach!"

---

  * Lincoln used this as an endearing term.

  † It cannot be known what form, or forms, of speech defect Tad Lincoln had. Lincoln authors have called it by various names.

KANSAS-NEBRASKA ACT
1854

The great triumvirate of Webster, Clay
And John Calhoun was dead. The younger set
Now strove for place and power. The Party's pet
Was Stephen Douglas, yearning for the day
When votes would make him President. One way
Seemed sure—his power as orator, to get
Some act through Congress that would surely fret
Debate, and by that art to win the fray!
Friends pointed out an issue thought to pave
His path— "Nebraska-Kansas Act,"* as planned,
Would catch all votes. They shrewdly would divide
The tract in two, each part to choose if slave
Or free. Men deemed this opened Northwest land
To slaves, and Congress sat well mystified.

---

* If a Democrat was to win the Presidency, he must win the South. Since Douglas was chairman of the Committee on Territories, he was in a position to steer such a course, and so the Kansas-Nebraska Bill was reported[67] to the Congress in January 1854.

MISSOURI COMPROMISE REPEAL
1854

Men knew, if passed, this Bill* would void the old
Missouri Compromise that long had eased
The strife between the North and South—appeased
Their fears of war. So, like a bomb, this bold
And controversial Act had shocked the hold
Of faith in man throughout the land; had breezed
Through flaming headlines as the press had pleased.
As Lincoln read, his blood ran hot and cold.

He stood in Champaign's courtroom when the news
First came, and questioned *why this Bill* was *brought
To vote,* since Douglas praised the Compromise!
Now, if this measure passed,† free men must lose!
Abe, tense, read all the papers through; then, sought
New goals—resolved to *save* this legal prize.§

---

* The Kansas-Nebraska Bill.

† Never had the brilliant Douglas oratory so gripped his listeners. After an all-night debate, the Bill finally passed the Senate at about five o'clock in the morning.[68]

§ The Missouri Compromise had been the *prize* National enactment for thirty-four years. But now, *if* it was to be *saved,* either this Senate-passed Kansas-Nebraska Bill had to be defeated in the House, or the principle of the Missouri Compromise would have to be *re*-established otherwise.

BACK IN POLITICS
1854

Thus politics claimed Lincoln once again,
And he campaigned for Yates,* a loyal son
Who had opposed the Kansas Bill. Since none
Had better qualities as citizen,
Abe urged that Yates be re-elected when
They cast their votes. All liked what Abe had done,
For Yates did almost make it, having won
New votes and confidence from freedom's men.

The Lincoln whom they heard was not the same
They knew as Congressman in 'forty-eight:
His growth had flowered in argument; aflame
With eloquence, he spoke with power and weight;†
His perfect English phrases brought acclaim—
In him, they glimpsed "a future man of state."

---

* Richard Yates.

† Lincoln opposed the Kansas-Nebraska Act; Douglas was strong for it, and continually preached his doctrine of Popular Sovereignty. They often spoke in the same towns, on the same day, and from the same platform.

THE LOST SPEECH
May 29, 1856

At Bloomington a tall man took the floor . . .
Then came a most momentous, tenseful hour
As Lincoln spoke with weird, hypnotic power.
Emotions rose from depths unknown, to pour
Through voice and phrase, as none had heard before.
The people sat enthralled awaiting flower
Of artistry, till climax built a tower
Of thought that lifted all on wings to soar.

Among the throng were men sent from the press,
Who were so rapt by Lincoln's magic spell
That they forgot to write out their report,
And lost to all the world was that address!*
But etched upon men's minds still rose and fell
Abe's plea, like music from some royal court.

---

* Because "no complete and authentic record of what may have been his greatest speech has ever been found", this address has since been referred to as the "lost speech." But the speech did weld the assembled multifarious and discordant factions of anti-Nebraska editors and politicians into a vigorous Republican Party in Illinois.[69]

LINCOLN ENTERS THE SENATORIAL RACE
1854-1855

Abe sought a Senate seat in 'fifty-four:[*]
Three candidates contended for the place;
At first, Abe led, then Matteson gave chase.
Since Trumbull was Abe's partisan,[†] to score
For free soil, Abe urged all the Whigs to pour
Their votes to Trumbull's aid, to win the race.
This, Lincoln's sacrifice for free-soil base,[70]
Let Lyman Trumbull enter victor's door.
Because the old Missouri Compromise
That Stephen Douglas managed to repeal
Was uppermost in this hard-fought campaign,
And Abe resolved to save that treasured prize,
All through the autumn months Abe spoke with zeal[§]
And urged the free-soil rights they must regain.

---

[*] The election took place in the State Legislature, for to become United States Senator from Illinois in those days the candidate had to be elected by the State Legislature, rather than by the people at large.

[†] While Lincoln was a Whig and Trumbull a Democrat, *both* were *anti-Nebraska partisans,* which Matteson was not.

[§] Lincoln's speeches commanded more marked attention than ever before.

LINCOLN AND INDUSTRY
1850-1860

Industrial development had brought
Great change to man in methods everywhere.
It bound the West to East with rails,* to snare
The river trade. The telegraph had taught
How man should value time in sending thought
By wire. Machinery had come to share
Man's work on farms, in factories; and chair
And sleeper railway-cars were being wrought.

Men meet such changing times when they adjust,
As Lincoln did. He made each speaking date
And Circuit Court by train. The railroads thrust
New cases in his hands to litigate.
They gave him good retainer fees; august
Decisions from his reasonings still rate.†

---

* In 1849-1857, almost 17,000 miles of track were laid, chiefly in the North where businessmen and farmers were turning to Eastern markets rather than to New Orleans.

† It was from a Railroad, the Illinois Central, in its court battle with McLain County, that Lincoln received a total fee of $5,000 for having won, in the State Supreme Court, an exceptionally vital decision of far-reaching importance.[71]

LINCOLN AND THE WEST

The democratic spirit stirred all men
To do great things: to work and share and be
A voice to rule the land, own home with tree
And yard, and worship God as heart may yen.
When land that reached to Mississippi's glen
Was opened up, it filled most rapidly
With talent, brain and aims of high degree,
Which met the needs of statesmen-citizen.*

Among the great who made the West well known
Was Harrison, the soldier-president,
And Clay, whose Compromise had clearly shown
Its worth; and Douglas, oratory-bent;
And last, Abe Lincoln, chief of all, we own,
Who made his faith in freedom permanent.

---

* The West, or what was the Northwest Territory, began to be a vital part of the nation as early as 1815-1820. It was also a political force to be reckoned with. Its population was (by the *World Almanac*) 2,600,000 in 1820, and 8,783,809 in 1860.

LINCOLN'S LEGAL EXPANSION
1857

The more Abe studied law, the greater grew
His practice—now it ranked among the best.
He tried all kinds of cases. With his zest
For searching minds of men, their vim and view,
He gained a richer goal than books imbue.
The railroads brought more cases without rest,
An I. C. suit he won was left as test
For other cases smiliar and new.

While not a corporation lawyer, he
Took bank and merchant cases, felt a thrill
To plead infringement for some patentee.
His *Afton*-Railroad case is cited still.*
Each murder case, like Armstrong's tragedy,
Is well recalled today for legal skill.

---

* The *Effie Afton* steamboat, on May 6, 1856, crashed into and destroyed a pier of the newly constructed railroad bridge that spanned the Mississippi River at Rock Island. The ship and cargo burned and sank, and the steamboat company sued the railroad company.

Lincoln was engaged to defend the railroad and the case came to trial in 1857. The far-reaching significance of this case was that it arrayed sections, eras and economies one against the other—north-south river route *vs.* east-west rail route, steamboat age *vs.* railroad age, markets of the South *vs.* markets of the North.[72]

McCORMICK-MANNY CASE
Cincinnati, 1854

The big McCormick case,* all will agree,
Has left important rulings to assay.
Abe Lincoln was engaged with an array
Of Eastern legal minds, at handsome fee.
Abe made research both wide and long to be
Assured of every angle, so to stay
Opponent's arguments set up to sway
Decisions of the judge, eventually.

The case was called,† but when Abe stood within
The group, vain Stanton ridiculing said,
"Get rid of him, for I cannot afford
Association with an 'ape'!"[73] Chagrin
Sank deep, for Lincoln *heard,* and bowed his head—
The gibe had pierced him like a thrust of sword.

---

* Cyrus H. McCormick sued John H. Manny for $400,000 for alleged infringement of a patent right on a mechanical reaper. Lincoln was retained to defend Manny. Lincoln's colleagues were George Harding of Philadelphia and Edwin M. Stanton of Pittsburg.

† The case was moved from Chicago to Cincinnati.

LINCOLN CHIVALRY
1854

The lawyers for McCormick‡ came to greet
The Manny legal men at court, but none
Gave Abe more than a nod! Again Abe's sun
Was dimmed. He felt that Stanton meant to cheat
Him of his place—make his rebuff complete,
For Lincoln understood he was the one
Engaged with *right to summarize* when done
With argument, still Stanton showed conceit.

"I have my brief prepared, sir," Lincoln said,
"But since we can't both close, you take my place."
Defiant Stanton shot, "I *will!*"* and led
The lawyers from the room, to shun Abe's face.
And—Abe? He sat with listeners instead,†
And watched the skill of Stanton win the case.§

---

‡ Edward M. Dickerson of New York and Reverdy Johnson of Baltimore.

* *See first* reference in *Addendum Note 73*.

† Lincoln saw the mastery of these Eastern lawyers and went home determined to study harder. *See second* reference in *Addendum Note 73*.

§ Including a $500 retainer fee, the Manny Company paid Lincoln a total of $2,000, which he divided equally with his law partner, William H. Herndon, reporting that Stanton had handled him roughly. *See first* reference in *Addendum Note 73*.

REPUBLICAN PARTY ORGANIZED
May 29, 1856

The slave discussion wrought a dread decay
Among the Whigs. The North was helplessly
Divided into groups; among them three,
With anti-Kansas views, designed to stay
The Compromise as legal power. One way
Was clear to all, and that was unity.
If all these parties could but once agree
To vote as one, there should be no delay.

Then came the merge, decreed— "Republican."*
And Frémont† was its choice for President.
He failed to win election, but no man
Felt greater pride in grand experiment.
The Party saw its gain, and then began
To build its future with a new content.

---

* Members of the Illinois-Bloomington Convention had urged Lincoln to attend the Philadelphia Convention where he received 110 votes for nomination as National Vice-Presidential candidate.

† John C. Frémont, whose work as a Free-Soiler had helped to bring California into the Union as a Free State.

DUFF ARMSTRONG'S TRIAL
1858

In May of eighteen fifty-eight, word came
To Lincoln as he drove through Circuit rut,
That young "Duff" Armstrong,[*] Hannah's son, was shut
In jail on murder charge. The Armstrong name
Drew Lincoln's sympathy. Duff was the same
That Abe had rocked while Hannah kindly cut
And sewed some patches on Abe's pants. Their hut
Was home to Abe. "How could Duff bring such shame?"

Abe took the case for Hannah's sake when told,
"My Duff is blamed for Metzker's[†] death. They'd been
On drinking sprees." One witness[§] said, "Duff's bold!
I saw him do it by moonlight!" Abe's chin
Went set: "Your testimony cannot hold!
There was no moon at twelve—your claims are thin!"[74]

---

[*] William "Duff" Armstrong, son of Jack and Hannah of New Salem. Jack had died and Hannah had to meet her son's accusation alone.

[†] James Preston Metzker of Beardstown, who was said to have been attacked in a drunken brawl at a camp meeting near Mason City.

[§] The witness was Charles Allen and the State's Attorney was Hugh Fullerton; Judge James Harriot presided.

LINCOLN ADDRESSES THE JURY
1858

Abe proved by almanac that none could see—
The moon had almost set. Abe brought one who
Had cast away the slung-shot,* telltale clue.
"That Metzker youth was drunk," Abe said, "and he
Fell off his horse three times, with injury
Enough to cause his death, as all of you
Know now! Yes, Duff is wild, but could not do
A thing that bad! His guilt could never be!"

The jurors heard Abe tell when that same lad
Lay in his cradle that Abe's own boot-toe
Would rock. And—there's his mother! Duff's not bad—"
Abe pled, with voice choked up. The long front row
Of jurors saw Abe's tears and filed out sad,
Then filed back in: "Not guilty, let him go!"[75]

---

* A piece of metal fastened to a strap to twirl, which Duff was accused of using.

HOW LINCOLN'S REPUTATION GREW

The Armstrong case revealed Abe's art homespun,
But sure. His Circuit cases had high rate,
His big Chicago practice, with the State
Supreme Court, showed percentage, lost and won,
To rank Abe with the lawyers topped by none:
A man revered for keen and legal weight,
By colleagues' and by Judges' estimate;
All prized the course his eager feet had run.

Today, you ask: "How could he do so *well*—
Perfect his English, Law and speech? His mind
Was never idle! Not a college bell
Rang out his fame, but records left behind
Have proved tenacity and work can spell
Success for all—if each has *will to grind.*

---

* Lincoln ranked among the best lawyers in a state that boasted of its outstanding legal talent.

A FULL YEAR— "JUDGE" LINCOLN
1856

Perhaps no year, as yet, had made demand
On Lincoln's thought and time like 'fifty-six.
He made some fifty speeches, sought to mix
All anti-slave men into one big band;
Campaigned for Frémont, bolstered up his stand
In Michigan; and served in politics.
He beautified his yard with walls of bricks,
Remodeled house and lawn as had been planned.

When Davis, Judge of Courts of Sangamon,[*]
Bade Lincoln serve the Courts as "Circuit Judge,"[76]
He saw that Lincoln's will to carry on
Would lift him from the lawyer's daily drudge.
Decisions Lincoln made were paragon
And stood all legal tests that left no grudge.

---

[*] David Davis, Judge of the Eighth Judicial Circuit. Lincoln also served later as "Judge" in four other counties.

LINCOLN VOTED SENATORIAL CANDIDATE
June 16, 1856

Republican Convention, 'fifty-eight,
Had met in Springfield. Since no single name
Within the past four years had won the fame
That Lincoln's had, as leader of his state,
It voted Abe its Senate candidate.*
Abe sensed the Douglas Presidential aim
Of preaching "sovereign rights"—a vote-get game
That Lincoln had resolved to terminate.

Abe smiled acceptance—made reply in speech:
"'A house divided . . . cannot stand',"† he said,
"Cannot remain 'half slave . . . half free.'† Man's reach
Through vote can make it free or further spread
The slave extensions. I implore—beseech
You think and vote with care to rid slave dread."

---

* The Illinois State Convention, by acclamation, passed a resolution that "Abraham Lincoln is the first and only choice of the Republicans in Illinois for the United States Senate as the successor of Stephen A. Douglas."

† Lincoln's own words, in quote marks within quote marks.[77]

THE GREAT DEBATE
1852-1858

No chapter in our nation's history
Has ever held so great significance
As Congress wrote in politics' advance,
From 'fifty-two and on, continually.*
What Congress does in our Democracy
But represents the nation's vote-expanse,
For acts are well discussed, in stores and manse,
On farms and streets, until most men agree.

Two strong forensic giants, set at bay,
Were each regarded great as orator.
These patriotic two proved worth each day
By wit and logic, leaving neither blur
Nor doubt on any point till all could say,
"They make the matter clear, and we concur."

---

* From 1852, two elements were warring over the extension of slavery. One was the Democratic-controlled Congress, and the other was the mass of people who resented or desired extension of slavery into "free-soil" territory.

POLITICAL FORENSIC GIANTS
1858

These giants lived in Illinois, and lo!
Within the fierce campaign of 'fifty-eight,
They both sought Senate seat. Each candidate
Was qualified, and both had hoped to show
Efficiency. Steve Douglas' speech held glow
And polish other speakers could not rate.
Yet, Lincoln bravely challenged him debate,
In districts round about, come weal or woe.

And thus the Lincoln-Douglas[*] argument
Was heard in seven towns.[†] The strong acclaim
Made millions read, and thousands were intent
On clearing views by witnessing the game
As played by these forensic giants, lent
To educate a nation's thought and aim.

---

[*] The two forensic giants were Abraham Lincoln and Stephen A. Douglas. Lincoln advocated no further extension of slavery, while Douglas proclaimed his Popular Sovereignty doctrine.

[†] Their debates were held in the following towns of Illinois: Ottawa, Freeport, Jonesboro, Charleston, Galesburg, Quincy and Alton. *See map, p. 32a, this volume.*

DOUGLAS TRAVELS IN STYLE

Steve Douglas traveled in a private car,[78]
His "Special" gayly dressed with flags and signs.
Stenographers were there to write his lines,
And secretaries who could quickly bar
From him "the vulgar throng." His wife, a star
Of beauty, traveled with him. "Now, no wines,"
She said. "Let adulation build your shrines!
The people all adore you, near and far!"

A flat held Douglas' cannon, myrmidon
In uniform would fire as if to say,
"Bring out your band for 'Doug' is coming on!"
But Lincoln rode the selfsame train that day
As common passenger, all sweaty—wan,
Along with others there without display.

THE PEOPLE ARE AROUSED
1858

They came—whole families, in wagons, carts,
On foot, on horse, from near and far, through dust,
To hear the subject uppermost discussed.*
Some groups brought food, while others bought at marts.
They waited hours while children munched their tarts.
And each man gave his views, with much disgust
Toward those who held beliefs they could not trust;
Republics thrive where freedom rules men's hearts.

And then, with roar of cannons, crowds appeared—
To fill the grounds, and horns began to blow
To greet the speakers, while the people cheered
And brass bands played as girls marched to and fro
And sang "America." The throngs then neared
The platform for the oratory flow.†

---

* *See Addendum Note 79* for New York newspaper report showing interest in these debates.

† The Midwest population was 8,783,809 by the 1860 census (as given in the *World Almanac*), while the population of the United States for that year was shown to be 31,443,321.

THE FREEPORT DOCTRINE
August, 1858

"The *central* government has highest right,"
Abe said, "to draft and pass these laws." This view
Was held by voters in the North, while through
The South men claimed the *state* held greatest might.
This variance had soon provoked the fight
Regarding slave advance within the new-
Made territories of the land; it grew
By war of words, and brought each side to light.

Then, Abe and Douglas met in "quiz" debate
At Freeport. Abe knew well of Steve's sly game:
To stand for what the voters advocate.
Abe asked, "Are territory laws the same
Concerning slaves as are those of the state?"
Steve's quick assent dimmed all his future fame.*

---

* Douglas needed only the Illinois vote to hold his seat in the Senate, and so he answered Lincoln according to the view held by his Illinois voters, which view was contrary to both his Popular Sovereignty doctrine and the Democratic view.[80]

VICTORY IN DEFEAT
1858

Though Douglas won election and regained
His Senate seat,* his lack of loyalty
To partisans† estranged the South till three
Small groups emerged,§ while Lincoln's views attained
More converts everywhere. Abe's mind was trained
In vision, shrewdness and proficiency,
In depth of logic plus its mastery.
Thus Lincoln's fame increased, while Douglas' waned.

At first, these great debates held eye and ear
Of men and press because of Douglas' view,
And oratoric flow—without a peer.
But soon, most hearers sensed that of these two
The stronger man was Lincoln— Abe could steer
The Ship of State in spite of gales that blew.

---

* Lincoln had won a majority of the popular vote throughout Illinois, but since the Legislature of Illinois then had final vote, which body due to gerrymander was controlled by Democrats, Douglas was returned to the United States Senate by a majority of eight over Lincoln.

† Southern Democrats.

§ The Seceders, the Unionists, and the Popular Sovereignty group.

LINCOLN
BECOMES
LEADER OF A DIVIDING PEOPLE

THE LINCOLN PHILOSOPHY

The Lincoln-Douglas race for Senate seat
Was done, and Lincoln—lost!* "It is no crime
To lose," Abe mused. He sensed a mental grime
That sheer fatigue had wrought, but could not cheat
His will and courage to press on. Like wheat
In golden head, Abe saw his fields at prime
And asked, "Who has not lost in tests of time?
Is there a man who has not known defeat?"

His vision pictured steep hillsides ahead
He must yet scale to win a place and be
Of aid in framing laws for right, and spread
Their truth to lift the land from slavery.
His vow to *reach* the *heights* where vision led
Brought faith and zeal to climb undauntedly.

---

* But while he had lost a Senate seat, the Lincoln-Douglas debates had made Lincoln a national figure and a logical candidate for President in 1860.

A LATE AUTUMNAL WALK
November, 1858

The prairie, lilac twilight was sublime
As Lincoln's gaze stretched to the firmament
Across the rolling reaches till it blent
With sinking sun. He heard the cowbells' chime,
Lambs' bleating, prairie chickens' coo . . . like rhyme,*
Across the prairie land where had been spent
His gift of latter days and mind had lent
Its force, out where was rest from mental climb.†

He walked beyond the town to be alone
And think apart from eager crowds that met
Him every day for months— "The blood and bone
Of our Democracy," he thought. "Man's debt
Has not been paid to such as these who own
This land; nor should we leave a slave, to fret!"

---

* These pastoral voices were like an idylic poem to soothe Lincoln's nerves.

† He had spent four months campaigning for a seat in the Senate, and with the added strain of the seven debates, he was in need of rest. At no time had he worked harder, and yet it seemed to him that all he had to show for it was his dwindled finances.

RETRIEVING LOSS
November, 1858

The office clock had struck the midnight hour.
The dust, that gathered from four months just gone,
Lay deep on legal papers that anon
Would get his care. Here lay the needed power
To help rebuild his bank account to flower
Again, to meet his family's need. Since dawn
His thoughts had sorted files, like questing fawn
That seeks to find its way through tangled bower.

He sorted cases, old from new, and filed
Each case for Circuit Courts. These fully claimed
His days, while speaking dates at night beguiled
His listeners till both increased. His famed
Debates with Stephen Douglas now had styled
Abe Lincoln, "orator." Thus laurels flamed.

LINCOLN DISCOVERED
1859

All summer many invitations came
For Abe to speak along the Eastern coast,
And West, where Minnesota* would be host.
His big Ohio welcome added fame
To Indiana praise and strong acclaim
Arising from Wisconsin's prideful boast:
"Abe Lincoln's speech at our State Fair was toast
Of all, and—ever since—his honors flame!"

Then Kansas planned his tour within their gate:
He spoke at Doniphan and Atchison,
At Troy and Leavenworth— The very date
John Brown was hanged, Abe warned, "If men would shun
Brown's end, then they must see before too late
That freedom can and must *by vote* be won."

---

* He accepted the October 1859 invitation to speak in February of 1860 at Cooper Union in New York City. He also accepted other invitations on the East coast, but declined the Minnesota invitations.

HENRY WARD BEECHER'S INVITATION
October, 1859

An invitation came from Plymouth Church.*
The Beecher name thrilled Abe, yet left much gloom
And doubt, for fear his cultural lacks would doom
The Beecher trust. Abe faced the truth, "This smirch,"
He vowed, "I must remove! As bird on perch
Seeks food for strength to soar above cloud-loom,
So must I seek for facts to disentomb
A scholarly address through wide research."

He studied well our Constitution's mold
And sought to learn each Founding Father's view
On spread of slavery, which questing told†
A clear majority opposed and knew
That Congress would control—thus we should hold
And bring to pass their dreams, and prove them true.

---

* Brooklyn's Plymouth Church, Henry Ward Beecher, pastor, later complied with Lincoln's wish that he be allowed to speak on some political subject and accordingly transferred sponsorship to a political group.

† Lincoln spent four months in search of historical documents, roll calls and quotations which he used to prove that at least 21 of the 39 signers of the Constitution, together with those of the 76 Congressmen who passed its first ten amendments, held the same view as the Republican Party on restricting slavery, intended no limitations on Congress pertaining thereto, and aimed "to exclude from the Constitution the idea that there could be property in man." [81]

AT COOPER UNION
February 27, 1860

At last the date for Lincoln's speech was set.
It took two days to reach New York, where he
Was entertained as *a celebrity!**
A snow fell all the day, the streets were wet
With melting, trickling, gurgling rivulet;
His carriage wheels, steel-tired, rolled noisily
And stopped at Cooper Union.† One could see
A waiting throng within, by arched gas jet.

His escort§ led him up the aisle, mid cheer;
The men upon the platform greeted him,
And William Cullen Bryant's strong, sincere,
Poetic words presented Abe. A glim
Of awkward silence charged the atmosphere
As Abe began. His speech then grew in vim.

---

* At the Astor House, arrayed in a handsome new black suit.
† The Young Men's Central Republican Union had taken the sponsorship of Lincoln's address, which was given in Cooper Union hall, New York City.
§ David Dudley Field, a prominent young attorney.

THE COOPER UNION SPEECH
February 27, 1860

Abe gave the Founding Fathers' view: how they
Had disapproved extending slavery.
The South's rejection of this policy
Had caused much agitation. "Many say
Their principles are just, that slaves should stay—
Who will not heed, theirs is the perfidy!"
Abe paused, and then in tense tones asked, "Shall we
Submit to them—yield truth to wrong—obey?

When duty calls, should not all heed command?
Today 'let us have faith' in moral right
'And in that faith,' O, 'let us . . . dare'* to stand!"
These closing words stirred all to such a height
The crowd arose, it cheered, then sought his hand,
And shouted long hurrahs in sheer delight.†

---

* Lincoln's own words, in quote marks within quote marks.[82]

† Lincoln made a profound impression on the press as well. Four New York newspapers printed his speech in full. The *Chicago Tribune* printed the speech in pamphlet form, and newspapers all over the country carried excerpts.

RECOGNIZED LEADERSHIP
1860

No speeches since the days of Webster, Clay,
Had stirred men's thinking more convincingly*
Than Lincoln's had, though charged with charity
For those at fault. Committees begged him stay
To lecture in the East, along the bay.
In Concord, Dover, Hartford, Norwich, he
Addressed great throngs. Men met in rhapsody,
With bands and much political display.

New York's acknowledged leaders could well make
A man, or kill his chance.† This, Lincoln knew;
But all were won by Abe. "He's no mistake—
He is today's most trusted man, whose view
Is safe," they sensed. "His level head can break
All opposition down and lead us through!"

---

* The New England newspapers praised Lincoln's speeches as the most powerful, logical and compact ever heard.

† When Lincoln returned to Illinois, he was warmly greeted. It meant much to his friends to have him crowned with the praises of the East's newspapers and to be introduced by the eminent poet, William Cullen Bryant, editor of the New York *Evening Post*.

EVENTS CAN CREATE A PRESIDENT
August 8, 1860

The Lincoln speeches carried in the press
Throughout the East were copied everywhere.
His home press and his friends were all aware
Events these past two years had served to dress
Abe up for President. In humbleness
He stood before men, hearing trumpets blare
And neighbors' praise proclaimed in prideful air.
Each saw in Abe's slight bow, his true *noblesse*.*

"Sir, we're assured," said Hay,† "we'll look in vain
For one more fit to meet the time and place
And the occasion than yourself. Our need
Is leaders in our land, with reason's reign."
Abe bowed in modesty, then stared in space
And thought, *"I must be led, if I would lead!"*

---

* Lincoln's deep humility was one of his most commendable traits, yet too often others mistook it for weakness.

† Milton Hay, Chairman of the Republican Committee, who introduced Lincoln with almost these very words at a rally held in Springfield, August 8, 1860, with 50,000 in attendance.

"LINCOLN, THE RAIL-SPLITTER"
May 9-10, 1860

The State Republican Convention met
Down at Decatur,‡ Lincoln's old home town.
Abe's friends recalled some deeds that gave renown
To early feats long past— "lest men forget."
Dick Oglesby* had plans that were well set:
John Hanks† should bring a banner in—hung down
Between two rails—inscribed, RAIL-SPLITTER, crown
Of slogans, aimed to serve as voter net.

The crowd went wild, it laughed, it yelled and cheered
Until the tent's roof-stays split overhead.§
Men thought the slogan great. Debris all cleared,
They asked that Lincoln speak. He rose and said,
"I cannot swear these rails are mine!" He peered
And smiled, "I have mauled better for my bread!"

---

‡ For pre-convention events, *see Addendum Note 83*.

* Richard Oglesby, later governor of Illinois.

† Lincoln's cousin, who had brought the Lincolns to Illinois in 1830, and had split rails with Abe.

§ The big tent wigwam was set up behind what is now the Millikin National Bank, as an auditorium for the State Convention of the Republican Party. A bronze tablet now marks the spot.

PRESIDENTIAL CANDIDATE
May 10, 1860

Next day Judge Palmer's* resolution read:
"Since Illinois Republicans decree
Abe Lincoln run for President, now be
It here resolved that delegates should spread
His worth, all *vote as one,* nor get misled
At National Convention† . . . all to see
Abe made Republicans' one nominee!"
"Unanimously passed," the chairman said.

The meeting broke in pandemonium.
The crowds had faith in Abe. The knew him well
And felt him safest man in days to come—
If peace or war—a man few could excel.
That night none slept, but marched with beat of drum
And playing bands, hurrahs, and clang of bell.

---

* Judge John M. Palmer of Macoupin County, a former Democrat turned Republican by his aversion to the Kansas-Nebraska Act.

† The Republican National Convention was held in Chicago, May 16-18, six days after the State Convention in Decatur.

NATIONAL REPUBLICAN CONVENTION
May 16-18, 1860, Chicago

Chicago had been chosen as the place
To hold the National Republican
Convention.* There, was drawn the caravan
Of delegates, with thousands more to brace
Each candidate. Abe Lincoln, Bates and Chase,
McLean, with Cameron and Seward ran;
But as the second balloting began,
Four men no longer counted in the race.

In Springfield, Abe and friends in rendezvous
Sat by the telegraph to hear it run
Its messages as each came pouring through,
With noisy clicking sound, till all were done.
Two ballots had been cast when all there knew
A third would prove if Abe or Seward† won.

---

* Chicago erected a pine-board wigwam to seat 10,000 which proved too small. New York sent 2,000, Pennsylvania 1,500, and the Midwest many thousands more.

† William H. Seward was the recognized leader of the Republican Party. Illinois Republicans knew he would be hard to beat, but all worked diligently in tense suspense.

LINCOLN NOMINATED FOR PRESIDENT
May 18, 1860, Chicago

The wires in ballot three heaped high the pile,
Reports came in so fast. All, tense, sat there
To learn if Abe or Seward won! Aware
Abe's chances grew, a quartette sang the while.
Then—came a wire—[*] One read it with a smile:
"Abe Lincoln's won!"[†] Abe gasped, "Now I must share
The news with Mrs. Lincoln who will care."[84]
His friends hurrahed and cheered in rally style.

And neither Springfield nor Chicago slept
That night. The people marched and sang, bands played,
Men hugged each other, cheered with glee, or wept!
Some yelled and others in the churches prayed;
Nor did the daylight, as it slowly crept
To view, dispel the joy of cannonade!

---

[*] The entire vote was 466; necessary to choice, 234; Lincoln, 354. The nomination was then made unanimous, amid intense excitement, on motion of William M. Evarts of New York.

[†] Diplomacy, strategy, and genuine admiration for Lincoln had won. Norman Judd had astutely secured the Convention for Chicago, and it was he who nominated Lincoln there. Chief strategist David Davis was ably assisted by Jesse Fell, Leonard Swett, Stephen T. Logan, Richard Oglesby, Joseph Medill, Orville Browning, Richard Yates, John M. Palmer, and others.

LINCOLN OFFICIALLY NOTIFIED
May 19, 1860

Next day, a group of politicians came
Confirming Abe's election, glad to free
Their minds of gnawing curiosity.
Their Chairman Ashmun,* heart and mind aflame,
Began: "This letter, sir, reveals our aim
To leave some words expressing faith's decree."
Then Ashmun paused, and Lincoln feelingly
Replied in simple words that brought acclaim.

Abe's friendliness, his mind alert, his hand
In social clasp, his chosen words—and grace
With which he gave them—served to countermand
All adverse fears. They studied his kind face
And genial air. "Who could have made or planned
A better choice," one said, "for this high place?"†

---

* George Ashmun of Massachusetts.

† Later, to one of Lincoln's townsmen, George Boutwell, Governor of Massachusetts, remarked: "Why, sir, they told me he was a rough diamond. Nothing could have been in better taste than that speech." "Well, we might have done a more brilliant thing," commented Judge W. D. Kelley of Pennsylvania, "but we could certainly not have done a better thing."[85]

REPUBLICAN PLATFORM
1860

Republicans had drawn their platform thongs
Secure, opposing slavery's expanse,*
Corruption, Democrats' extravagance,
Secession—that alarmed like shrill fire gongs,
And "hotheads" in the South,† who urged these wrongs.
Republicans, thus armed, now sought their chance
With slogans, "Honest Abe," a safe advance,
"Rail-Splitter," that would win the vote of throngs.

Though Seward knew defeat, he took the stump
For Lincoln, while the other candidates
Supported eagerly their party trump.
These loyal men campaigned throughout the States;
United in their cause, it could not slump,
But grew in strength *to win the last debates.*

---

* As advanced by Stephen A. Douglas in his Popular Sovereignty doctrine.

† The Secession leaders were known as "hotheads." They were Robert B. Rett, South Carolina; James D. B. DeBow and John Slidell, Louisiana; Edmund Ruffin, Virginia; and William Lowndes Yancey, Alabama.

LINCOLN'S LOYAL FRIENDS

Abe Lincoln's advocates were men proved true,
Who trusted most Abe's shrewd sagacity,
His brilliant mind and careful mastery
Of party principles which would construe
As neither radical nor languid view.*
These men were legion, but some ten could see
Their party's need for them, that they agree
To act as speakers all the campaign through.

Such men were Judd and Fell, Medill and Swett,
With Logan, Yates and Davis strategists.
They made Abe's nomination sure, they met
Election needs and served as analysts.
Such friends and partisans none could forget,
Nor Seward, Schurz and Chase†—his votarists.

---

* Lincoln made no campaign speeches, while all the opposing candidates did.

† Norman B. Judd, Jesse W. Fell, Joseph Medill, Leonard Swett, Stephen T. Logan, Richard Yates, David Davis, William H. Seward, Carl Schurz, Salmon P. Chase.

DEMOCRATIC NATIONAL CONVENTION
1860

The Democratic Party now was split
In three. Not one could win, but all stood true.
All groups were sure that they were right and grew
Most arrogant and strove, with bulldog grit,
To prove the other groups were no more fit
To rule than were Republicans! Some knew
Extremists held *Secession* as their view,
And chose John Breckinridge, a man of wit.

Bell's Constitution Party would preserve
The *Union*—but *with slaves!* And Douglas still
Was preaching *Popular Sovereignty*.* With nerve
Of steel, he fought with words and virile will—
Abe's strongest rival—yet with all his verve
He lost to Lincoln's moral right and skill.

---

* While Stephen Douglas abhored secession, he opposed John Bell's claim that the Constitution authorized slavery. The Douglas doctrine of Popular Sovereignty would leave it to the people of each territory as to whether it would become a Free- or a Slave-State.

However, as the campaign progressed, Douglas is reported to have become convinced that " 'Mr. Lincoln is the next President. We must try to save the Union. I will go South.' His speeches there were fiercely Unionist . . . but it was his misfortune to be accounted proslavery in the North and antislavery in the South."[86]

LINCOLN'S STATE HOUSE OFFICE
Summer, 1860

Steve Douglas stumped through all the hot campaign,
But Lincoln sat in office and discussed
His views with party men, who sought his trust
And confidence for methods to make gain.
Abe's private secretaries[†] bore the strain
Of flooded mails, with grace or sheer disgust.
Meanwhile, an artist,[§] on his canvas, thrust
The Lincoln face, in sad or thoughtful vein.

Abe Lincoln knew each national event
And trend, and sensed just how he stood each day.
He met the callers[87] as they came and went;
Some came to gaze at him in sullen sway,
While others came to laud and leave content—
But of the thousands, none were turned away.

---

[*] During the summer and winter of 1860-1861, Lincoln moved his office to a room in the State House.

[†] John C. Nicolay was private secretary to Lincoln, with John Hay as his assistant.

[§] A number of artists came to paint Lincoln's portrait that summer and autumn; five biographies of Lincoln were also written.

CAMPAIGN IRONY

From Lincoln's nomination, and on through
Election, papers* limned him as grotesque—
An ape or big gorilla, at his desk.
This joshing spread as time ran on. Abe knew
Such was the usual test for all those who
Were in the public's eye: mere press burlesque
And party blasphemy in arabesque.
Abe smiled and chalked them up, "Campaigners' brew."

These days were busy ones for Abe. He met
Large throngs of men each hour, from everywhere;
And one of these was Thurlow Weed,† whose boast
Had been, "Bill Seward is my man!" And yet
Weed's mind was changed on meeting Abe, aware
That Lincoln *was the man* a world would toast.

---

* The newspapers of the three opposing parties.

† Editor of the *Albany Journal,* an excellent political boss, and the counselor and friend of William H. Seward; supported Lincoln to help make a place for Seward in Lincoln's cabinet.

CAMPAIGN DEMONSTRATIONS
1860

Conventions done, the chosen candidates
For President were four.* Each leading man
Was heralded at rallies which began
And closed the hot campaign. Nor were there waits
Until parades with speakers—party mates—
Were sounding virtues of the men who ran.
With glee clubs, torchlights, march of partisan,
They hoped to gain the vote that dominates.

These celebrations held the ear and eye
Of throngs who came from near and far to pay
Their homage due to our Republic, vie
For better leadership and thus display
Their party's cause. Thus, hopes were kept at high—
Through rallies that precede election day.[88]

---

* These four were John C. Breckinridge, John Bell, Stephen A. Douglas and Abraham Lincoln.

SPRINGFIELD RALLY
August 8, 1860

Of all the rallies of this hot campaign,
None drew such throngs or fostered more renown
Than did the one in Lincoln's own home town,*
Where fifty thousand persons sought to gain
The needed votes to clinch Abe Lincoln's reign.
The long two-mile procession, marching down
Eighth Street, passed Lincoln's home; their ranks of brown,
With bands, glee clubs and floats, thrilled heart and brain.

A little lad before a fire-lit book,
A man with axe and pile of rails well made,
A log house in a wood, debates that shook
The land, revealed "Old Abe" as life assayed.
Then came the speeches,† rally chants that took
The crowds by storm, their firm decisions stayed.

---

* Springfield, Illinois.

† Republican speakers were Cullom, Yates and Trumbull of Illinois, Carl Schurz of Wisconsin, Caleb Smith of Indiana and Zachariah Chandler of Michigan. There were five speaker's stands, with speakers on each being heard at the same time to accommodate the vast crowd.

A PLEDGE OF LOYALTY
August 8, 1860

As Lincoln stood to watch the long parade
That passed his house, he heard glad shouts of joy
And saw a group of college youth.* Each boy
Had stopped to choose a cane that had been made
From rails that "Abe had cut." His nod assayed
New confidence as each picked up his toy;
Aware of Lincoln's greatness, they were coy,
But Lincoln's smile encouragement conveyed.

One lad then asked, "Is this cane walnut hew
Or locust wood?" Abe studied nature's planned
Design, "Well, son, that cane is walnut, see?"
And glancing up he cried, "Why, James, it's you!"†
"Yes, Mr. Lincoln, from your own dear hand
I take this gift, and pledge my loyalty."§

---

* From Mt. Zion Academy, Mt. Zion, Illinois.

† Lincoln never forgot a face. The youth was James H. Crowder of Marrowbone. James confessed to the author that he knew the cane was walnut, but that he wished to take it directly from Lincoln's hand.

§ James fulfilled his pledge to Mr. Lincoln by leaving college and serving three years in the Union Army.[89]

ELECTION DAY
November 6, 1860

Abe sat alone upon a State House chair
Reviewing turbid scenes of months gone past
Since nomination, while his heart beat fast:
Buchanan's inactivity—* aware
That radicals were working everywhere . . .
Six States were planning to withdraw! Aghast,
Big-hearted friend to all, Abe felt fate's blast
And pled for peace; within his heart was prayer.

At three, Abe went to vote amid the cheer
Of crowds along the streets. His duty done,
He then walked home believing that the right
Would be revealed by vote. He longed to hear
The full returns come in, and yet no one
Had greater calm than Lincoln had that night.

---
* *See Addendum Note 90.*

"MARY, WE HAVE WON!"

Abe sought the telegraph where partisan
And friends had met to hear returns as they
Came sifting through from home and far away.
He had not long to wait for news began
To filter through, and then so swiftly ran
None could quite tabulate or dare assay
Which candidate would likely win the day,
Yet all felt Lincoln was the leading man.

Though Abe's election was most imminent,
No man was sure. With singing crowds outside,*
And hush within, suspense seemed punishment.
Then came the flash that gave the voting tide:
"Abe Lincoln is elected President!"[91]
"Oh, Mary, we have won!" Abe said with pride.

---

  * Singing a campaign song:
   "Aren't you glad you joined the Republicans,
   Joined the Republicans, joined the Republicans,
   Aren't you glad you joined the Republicans,
   Out in Illinois!"

SECESSION BEGINS
December 20, 1860

When Carolina,* Southern slave-pledged state,
December twentieth, with finished plan,
Had left the Union, other states began
To talk the same. Alarm then spread. Ornate
Newspapers' glaring headlines flamed: "The fate
Of traitors must be met![†] We'll firmly ban
Disunion, and put down this rebel clan!
The Union must be saved, nor should we wait!"

Not till more states seceded[§] did Abe's chin
Go set, nor did he lose his faith and trust
In them. He saw great need of discipline
Through reasoning; but when *they trailed through dust
The Nation's flag,* Abe knew all hope to win
Them back was gone, *yet hoped* they would adjust.

---

* South Carolina.

† Substance of comment by Edward L. Baker, editor of the *Illinois State Journal,* in Springfield.

§ Six more states to secede were Georgia, Florida, Alabama, Mississippi, Louisiana and Texas.

LINCOLN VISITS HIS STEPMOTHER
January 31, 1861

Perhaps no days were busier than those
Before the Lincolns went to Washington.
He let his house, sold furnishings, had done
His first inaugural address; he chose
The men to form his cabinet, met foes
As well as friends in each day's office run,
And rushed his work that he might have just one
Week end to visit kindred in repose.

He spent a day down on his father's farm*
With his stepmother who was living there.
He saw her pride in him, and her alarm
At national conditions. Deep in prayer,
They stood beside his father's grave: "Thine arm,
Dear God, enfold us here and everywhere!"

---

* Lincoln left Springfield on January 30, went to the farm on January 31, and arrived back at Springfield on February 1.

TREASON STALKED THE LAND
February 4, 1861

Grim treason's shadow stretched across the land
And spread its flaming terror instantly,
When those six states which favored slavery,
Seceded from the Union's treasure band.
They met in Alabama where they planned
And formed a slave combine that was to be
Known hence: Confederated States, per se;[*]
Jeff Davis, President, to take command.

They seized the arsenals and forts within
Their states, prepared for war—intent to mar
The Union. Hotheads cried, "The South can win!"
Buchanan,[†] weak and spineless, watched the spar,
Nor sought to quell; while Lincoln felt chagrin
And helplessness as treason stalked afar.

---

[*] The Southern Confederacy was formed in Montgomery, Alabama.

[†] James Buchanan, President of the United States.

LINCOLN'S LAST WALK

The Lincoln trunks were strapped, their boxes sent,
And Abe, in sunset's crimson hour, began
To walk the prairie fields he loved. There ran
Beside him Tad and Willie, who were bent
On chasing young wild gophers. This sport lent
Excitement to their walk. But Lincoln's ban
From mind of all thoughts save how best to plan
The trip to Washington, left discontent.

His faith in men was such, he thought to spurn
The need of *armed protection* through the long
Train trip, as his committee warned; pride's burn
Would humble him by thinking such a wrong!
Yet, as he walked, his good friends' deep concern
Brought calm submission like an evening song.

LINCOLN SENSES HIS TASK
February, 1861

The night had waned. In Springfield's best hotel*
Abe woke to hear the sparrows' cheery lay
That pierced the holy silence greeting day—
To Abe, life's matin hour. He felt the spell . . .
A calm against the flaming Rebel hell
That swept the land and threatened its decay.
No human eye could penetrate the way
Ahead. He sensed in this a warning knell.†

And Lincoln's spirit sought God's guiding light
To mark his unknown path, to help unmask
The blinded eyes of men whose ruthless might
Was perpetrating wrong. "Forbid, I ask,
And let them *see* and ever *will the right."*
Within his soul he sensed his giant task!

---

* The Lincolns stopped at the Chenery House for several nights before going to Washington.

† Political conditions were like a boiling volcano, threatening to erupt at any moment. Lincoln no doubt thought like others, that war was imminent.

THE GREAT WESTERN STATION*
February 11, 1861

The day was dark and chill, a drizzling rain
Came down, yet in the station waiting room
His friends were saying their good-byes. The gloom
Of separation felt by all, like pain
Of surgeon's knife, was deep and keen. None deign
Relate the *fears* he *sensed*. A nation's bloom
Had been despoiled by ruthless thrusts, till doom
Spread far its discontent, and hope seemed vain.

None felt the dangers lurking any more
Than Lincoln did; and none could then foretell
The years ahead. Amid the hiss and roar
Of steam he climbed the steps, as ringing bell
Clanged, "All aboard!" He walked back through the door
And stood,† head bared, to speak a last farewell.§

---

* The Great Western Railroad is now known as the Wabash.

† On the rear platform of the train.

§ It is estimated that the Springfield crowd assembled for his farewell was a thousand or more.

"AN AFFECTIONATE FAREWELL"[*]
February 11, 1861

Abe stood before them like a sturdy oak;
They crowded near to catch his voice and eyes.
He stood and waited for hurrahs and cries
To cease, and then, in simple speech, he broke
The heartache pause and eloquently spoke
His farewell words straight from his heart! His rise
And growth from small beginnings was a prize
Beyond their ken. New pride in him awoke.

Abe told them of the tasks that he must do,
Far greater than George Washington had manned:
"He did create, I must preserve his view
Whatever comes." He bade them "hold God's hand
And, knowing 'right makes might,' He'll see us through;
But without God we fail, we cannot stand!"

---

[*] Lincoln's own words. *See Addendum Note 92.*

This farewell is regarded as one of Lincoln's great speeches. Like all enduring oratory, it was an overflow of the heart couched in simple phrases.

THE TRAIN LEAVES SPRINGFIELD
8:20 A.M., February 11, 1861

The flag-draped train[*] began to move with steam
And clang of bell. Abe heard the last good-byes
And turned to join his son[†] and friends, while skies
Wept tears that flecked car windowpanes. A stream,
Awakened from its frozen winter dream,
Went babbling on as winds blew shrieking cries;
Then, clouds began to wing, like butterflies,
And let the heavens sift a gold sunbeam.

Within the station, friends said: "Now, he's gone!"
"His job is dangerous without a doubt!"
Another said, "Our Abe knows pro and con;
He's keen and reasons well, he's been about!"
Through curls of smoke the train sped swiftly on;
Each town- or crossroads-group hailed it with shout.

---

[*] The engine was decorated with fluttering flags. The two coaches and the baggage car were festooned in bunting of the national colors. The engine's headlights flared like the burning nostrils of Jupiter. And as Jupiter had rushed to protect law, justice and virtue, so did the "Lincoln Special" now rush through the land proclaiming justice.[93]

[†] Robert Lincoln.

ON LINCOLN'S INAUGURAL TRAIN

On this famed train* were men from Abe's own state
And other parts. Each made with Abe the run,
To hear him speak, and see, in Washington,
The grand inaugural. There were sedate,
Trim army men, and Bob,† with college mate;
Train officers and crew; a sleuth with gun;
Reporters wiring Lincoln's speeches—one
Or more a day, for papers to relate.

With these were Lincoln's secretaries, gay
But capable; two bodyguards on hand
If need, and good Doc Wallace close to stay
Disease. Since all these men were of one brand,
They sensed Abe's cause as right and dared assay
Its worth. Such men have made this nation stand.

---

* For list of persons on the Lincoln Inaugural train, *see Addendum Note 94.*
† Robert Lincoln, son of the President-elect.

NEARING DECATUR
9:24 A.M.

Abe sat beside the window in the train
And gazed, though seeing neither land nor sky;
He saw the Nation's youth march out to die
As sacrifice, if war should come! While vain
Buchanan hesitated with disdain
To stop secession, Abe could hear the cry
A nation gave for *action* as reply.
Thus Lincoln's thoughts ran on, like links of chain.

He heard the noise of grinding wheels resound
While rumbling through the woods among the hills
Across old Stevens Creek where he had spent
His strength,[*] cut rails, made his first speech and found
Law practice in Decatur Courts.[†] With thrills
His good friends *there* had named him President.[§]

---

[*] Four miles west of Decatur a preserve marks the place where the Lincolns' first Illinois homestead stood, which Abe helped to build.

[†] The log courthouse, in which Lincoln practiced law in Decatur, now stands in Decatur's Fairview Park. For a 21-year chronology of Lincoln's law cases in Decatur, *see Addendum Note 95.*

[§] A bronze tablet on the east end of Decatur's Millikin National Bank marks the spot where the Illinois Republican wigwam stood. *See map, p. 20, this volume.*

DECATUR STRONG FOR LINCOLN

The train slowed down and stopped.[96] Abe saw, outside,
Familiar faces midst the throng that milled
About awaiting him—all eager, thrilled
With glow of confidence. They stood moist-eyed
And reached to shake his hand, revealing pride.
He smiled, but when he spoke his voice was filled
With pathos, almost heartache tones unwilled
To be expressed, but etched too deep to hide.

He may have searched for "Uncle Bobby's" James,[‡]
With lads fresh from Mt. Zion's College hall.
He spoke to Gorin[*] and James Millikin,
To Ullrich and John Hanks,[†] and smiled acclaims
To waving women folks, and last of all
To Oglesby[§] who wore a happy grin.

[‡] Later, the Reverend James H. Crowder, Bethany, Illinois.

[*] Jerome K. Gorin, John Ullrich.

[†] "John Hanks [Lincoln's cousin] followed Lincoln to Washington and was there for the inauguration. He visited Lincoln at the White House. . ."[97]

[§] Richard J. Oglesby.

A MAN OF FRIENDS

Perhaps no man has ever had more friends
Than Lincoln had. His heart was such he grieved
To lose a single one, and thus achieved
Beyond most men. Sincerity defends
Its friendships loyally unto their ends;
Abe did not stoop to blandishment. Deceived,
He bore the painful brunt until relieved
By better understanding and amends.

At all the towns they passed, folks met his train:
In Illinois, and Indiana, too;
Ohio people even braved the rain
To see and hear him, wish him safely through;
New York[98] and Pennsylvania felt much gain
In Abe, who held their firm, prevailing view.

MARY LINCOLN REBELS

Since all democracies must operate
By means of classified or party vote,
These parties are of fundamental note.
The loss of rule by Democrats brought hate
Toward all Republicans, whose party weight
Had won the race. The losers sought the throat
Of opposition ranks, with threat and gloat
Of vengeance some had vowed to perpetrate.

Republican advisors felt a fear
For Lincoln and his family, lest they
Should not reach Washington. As time drew near
They deemed it best that Mrs. Lincoln stay
And *follow* Lincoln's train. Her ride was drear,
So *she rebelled* and joined Abe's train next day!*

---

* At Indianapolis, Indiana; together with the two small Lincoln sons accompanying her.

GIST OF LINCOLN'S SPEECH ENROUTE

The clamoring of men to see and hear
Their new-elected President was strong.
The trip to Washington was twelve days long—
By winding route,* that many men might clear
Their views with his. He sought to calm their fear,
To bring new faith that no secession-wrong
Could sever Union ties. Thus did the throng
Gain confidence to say, "Abe's safe to steer!"

Abe's greatest emphasis was his appeal
That this great *Union be preserved*: "I ask,
Can Presidents, though filled with earnest zeal,
Perform *your* work? It is *the people's task!*
Until the rebels charge, we'll seek to heal,
But should they strike, our guns we will unmask."

---

* Lincoln made speeches at Decatur, Indianapolis, Columbus, Cincinnati, Cleveland, Buffalo, New York, Trenton, Harrisburg and Philadelphia.

PLOT AND COUNTERPLOT

Secession burned with hate. Like coiled-up snake
Awaiting time to strike with aim to stun,
It hissed, "Abe Lincoln shan't reach Washington!"
Wild plots were made to wreck the train or make
More sure by pistol shot, but wide awake
Detectives learned that such a plan begun
Would crystallize *in Baltimore* and run
Until its thirst for venom, hate could slake.

But counterplot had planned a rush through town
Where change of train was made,* and thus arrive
Before the published scheduled time. With frown
And pistol cocked, Ward Lamon† did contrive
To take Abe through to Washington, to crown
The nation's honor, fouling hate's vile drive.

---

* *In Baltimore.*

† Ward Hill Lamon, one of Lincoln's bodyguards—a former law associate, agreed to see Lincoln safely through to Washington.

LINCOLN REACHES WASHINGTON
February 23, 1861

They planned that Lincoln take a sleeping car
To pass through rebel Baltimore at dead
Of night, with Lamon there beside his bed.
Much fear of lurking ills was felt afar;[*]
Hence, Allan Pinkerton, detective star,
Had planned protection, and to Felton[†] said,
"With Lamon there to guard, the Lincoln head
Is safe to reach its goal without a scar!"[99]

Thus Abe and Lamon left the "Special" then,
And took an early train that rapidly
Switched Lincoln's sleeping coach just as "Big Ben"[§]
Chimed two in Baltimore. Thus, victory!
The Lincoln coach reached Washington: for men,
A place of power; for Abe—Gethsemane!

---

[*] The United States had no Secret Service at that time.

[†] S. M. Felton, president of the Philadelphia, Wilmington and Baltimore Railroad.

[§] The town clock. The Lincoln coach arrived in Washington at dawn, the "Lincoln Special" some four or five hours later.

"THE LINCOLN SPECIAL" ARRIVES

By mid-forenoon the flag-decked train came in,
With Lincoln's many friends and family.
All Washington had met the train to see
Their President. Some there held views akin
To Lincoln's, some did not; all felt chagrin
When told that Lincoln, President-to-be,
Arrived at dawn. But mass psychology
Prevailed and gave a welcome genuine.

With journey done, the travelers felt they
Should seek release from strain in quiet rest,
So friends in carriages whisked them away
To some hotel.* In dreams they heard the West
And East again, in cheers and glad hurray
That had sped Lincoln's train upon its quest.

---

* Most of the party went to the Willard Hotel, where the best suite had been reserved for Lincoln and his family.

PRESIDENT BUCHANAN RECEIVES

Some men, whose courage braved the hard campaign
By stumping states for Lincoln everywhere,
Arrived in Washington and were aware
The contest must go on until their gain
Was goal. They called on Lincoln to obtain
His views, that with their own they might compare.
Some Senators, moreover, called to share
A social hour, each with high hat and cane.

Nine days* sped rapidly, with much achieved.
One afternoon the Lincolns paid respect
To President Buchanan and his niece.†
With courtesy and pomp they were received;
The Lincolns shrewdly wise in turn, deflect
All issues of impending war or peace.

---

* Lincoln arrived in Washington nine days before his inauguration, which occured March 4, 1861. Four months had run by since his election.

† President Buchanan was an aging bachelor. His niece, Miss Harriet Lane was "Lady of the White House."

PLANNING THE INAUGURATION

With plans for Abe's inauguration made,
The news-sheets then proclaimed them everywhere.
His party's National Committee there
Asked Lincoln's wishes for the grand parade.
"A simple one," he said. Thus plans were laid:
The Nation's flag alone, should float in air
Along the line of march. All were aware
That *honors due that flag, must* still *be paid*.[*]

Its gleaming stars, its red, its white and blue,
Could never wave against a sky more bright
Than when displayed along the Avenue.[†]
It still assured mankind, in troubled night,
That *God keeps watch above His own;* ensue
What may, His will must triumph over might.

---

[*] The dancing on the Stars and Stripes by the Secession actress, Maggie Mitchell, on tne occasion of the inauguration of Jefferson Davis as President of the Confederacy, had caused such shock and bitter resentment that all had become acutely aware of the respect due the flag.

[†] Pennsylvania Avenue.

NIGHT BEFORE INAUGURATION
March 3, 1861

The midnight hour had passed. Abe had not slept,
But while he dozed his mind lived fitful dreams:
A barefoot boy by winding, woodland streams,
Where childhood days were spent, and youth had crept
Up hills for grapes or hazelnuts, or stepped
The rock-bed shallows where the sunlight gleams
And beauty dances in its rippling beams.
These childhood memories, mind prized and kept.

Abe saw again his homemade trundle bed
Up in the loft, saw strong wall pegs to be
The steps to climb; saw loved ones, now long dead;
Then, semiconsciously he planned to free
And save the land . . . until the night had fled—
And, wide awake, Abe faced reality!

ADDENDA NOTES

These notes are included to give documentation and additional information, especially on associated background and controversial subjects.

p. 22 — n. 1 — Benjamin P. Thomas, *Abraham Lincoln: A Biography* (New York, Alfred A. Knopf, 1952), p. 21.
— n. 2 — Albert J. Beveridge, *Abraham Lincoln: 1809-1858* (Boston, Houghton Mifflin Company, 1928), Vol. I, p. 105; and Otto R. Kyle, *Abraham Lincoln in Decatur* (New York, Vantage Press, 1957), p. 33.

p. 23 — n. 3 — Josephine Craven Chandler, *New Salem: Early Chapter in Lincoln's Life* (Revised Edition, Reprint from *The Journal of the Illinois Historical Society,* Vol. 22, No. 4, January, 1930), pp. 10-11.

p. 24 — n. 4 — Charles H. Coleman, *Abraham Lincoln and Coles County: A Chronology* (Mimeographed, Charleston, Eastern Illinois University, 1956); and Ida M. Tarbell, *In the Footsteps of the Lincolns* (New York, Harper & Brothers, 1924), p. 167.

p. 25 — n. 5 — Chandler, *New Salem,* p. 10.
— n. 6 — Carl Sandburg, *Abraham Lincoln: The Prairie Years and The War Years* (one-volume edition: New York, Harcourt, Brace and Company, 1954), p. 23.

p. 26 — n. 7 — *Ibid.*

p. 31 — n. 8 — Benjamin P. Thomas, *Lincoln's New Salem* (Springfield, The Abraham Lincoln Association, 1934), p. 24.

Chandler, *New Salem,* p. 9, says, "John Cameron and his uncle, James Rutledge . . . established a mill that was both a grist and a saw mill upon the Sangamon at this point." Offutt bought a share in the mill and had Lincoln do some of the work there.

p. 33 — n. 9 — Sandburg, *Prairie and War Years,* pp. 29-31, states that Lincoln enlisted three times: the first time at Richland Creek, for 30 days, as captain; again at Ottawa, for 20 days, as a private, in Captain Elijah Iles' mounted Rangers; then, for another 30 days, in Captain Jacob M. Early's Spy Corps which was searching for Black Hawk and his warriors in hiding. Lincoln was mustered out at White Water on Rock River, July 10.

p. 34 — n. 10 — Harry E. Pratt, *Abraham Lincoln Chronology: 1809-1865* (Springfield, Illinois State Historical Library, 1953), p. 2.

p. 35 — n. 11 — Thomas, *Abraham Lincoln,* p. 36.

— n. 12 — Roy P. Basler, ed., Marion Dolores Pratt and Lloyd A. Dunlap, assist. eds., *The Collected Works of Abraham Lincoln* (New Brunswick, N. J., Rutgers University Press, 1953), Vol. IV, p. 65.

— n. 13 — Thomas, *Abraham Lincoln,* p. 37.

p. 36 — n. 14 — Pratt, *Chronology,* p. 2.

p. 37 — n. 15 — Sandburg, *Prairie and War Years,* pp. 27, 35.

p. 41 — n. 16 — Basler, ed., *Collected Works,* Vol. IV, p. 65.

— n. 17 — Pratt, *Chronology,* p. 3.

— n. 18 — Thomas, *Abraham Lincoln,* p. 40.

p. 42 — n. 19 — Pratt, *Chronology,* p. 3.

— n. 20 — Chandler, *New Salem,* pp. 40-41. *Cf.* Basler, ed., *Collected Works,* Vol. IV, p. 65.

p. 44 — n. 21 — Thomas, *Abraham Lincoln,* p. 45. Sandburg, *Prairie and War Years,* p. 41, states that Lincoln paid $60 for the new tailor-made suit he wore to Vandalia.

p. 46 — n. 22 — Tarbell, *Footsteps of Lincolns,* p. 217.

p. 47 — n. 23 — Thomas, *Abraham Lincoln,* p. 50.

p. 48 — n. 24 — Sandburg, *Prairie and War Years,* pp. 38-40, 46.

Addenda Notes

p. 49 — n. 25 — Thomas, *Abraham Lincoln*, p. 51, says "the story caught the popular fancy. Embellished by sentimental fiction-writers and dramatists, it became enshrined in American folklore . . . Thus came to culmination a legend for which no shred of contemporary evidence has been found. Nothing in Lincoln's writings support it."

p. 52 — n. 26 — William E. Barton, *The Life of Abraham Lincoln* (Indianapolis, The Bobbs-Merrill Company, 1925), Vol. I, pp. 205-210.

— n. 27 — Thomas, *Abraham Lincoln*, p. 62.

p. 53 — n. 28 — Barton, *Life of Lincoln,* Vol. I, p. 205; Pratt, *Chronology,* p. 3.

p. 55 — n. 29 — Pratt, *Chronology,* p. 3.

p. 56 — n. 30 — Thomas, *Abraham Lincoln,* pp. 75-76. *Ibid.,* pp. 76-77, also states that Springfield had six churches, a Young Men's Lyceum, a Thespian Society, an academy, a Temperance Society, and several private schools, and that such celebrities as the Swiss Bell Ringers, ex-President Van Buren, and Daniel Webster were heard there.

p. 58 — n. 31 — Lincoln was a busy man. He was still paying on the Lincoln-Berry store debt, and also on his frail father's farm. He needed money, but it was not his one aim. He had a law office in Springfield; and he also had law cases in Charleston and Urbana. He made political speeches for William Henry Harrison, Whig candidate for President, and was a representative in the Illinois Legislature.

p. 59 — n. 32 — The Democrats carried Illinois from 1838 to 1856. So Lincoln could not win a seat in the Electoral College, but as a candidate for that office he was permitted to make speeches for his party's candidate, and this he did for sixteen years. This kept him before the public and increased his popularity as a speaker. Pratt, *Chronology,* p. 3, says, "1839, Oct. 8. Lincoln is chosen one of the presidential electors by the Whig convention. He is likewise honored in 1844, 1852 and 1856."

p. 60 — n. 33 — *Ibid.,* "1839, Sept. 23. Lincoln begins practice on the newly organized Eighth Judicial Circuit. He continues to attend these courts until his nomination for the presidency."

p. 61 — n. 34 — Thomas, *Abraham Lincoln,* p. 92. While this was Lincoln's earnings per year by 1842, Harry E. Pratt, *The Personal Finances of Abraham Lincoln* (Springfield, Ill., The Abraham Lincoln Association, 1943), pp. 84-85, says that "between 1840 and 1850, Lincoln's annual income from the law was probably between $1,500 and $2,000" and that "Ninian W. Edwards who, as everyone was aware, lived well . . . admitted . . . that his living expenses . . . did not exceed $1,200 a year."

For further description of Lincoln's Circuit travels, *see* Ida M. Tarbell, *The Life of Abraham Lincoln* (four-volume edition: New York, The Lincoln History Society, 1895), Vol. II, pp. 35-50.

p. 64 — n. 35 — Ruth Painter Randall, *Mary Lincoln: Biography of a Marriage* (Boston, Little, Brown and Company, 1953), pp. 47-48, states that Ninian W. Edwards, Mary's brother-in-law and guardian, was radical, particularly, first, because Lincoln was log-cabin born, and second, because Lincoln advocated democracy rather than aristocracy. Lincoln broke the engagement on January 1, 1841.

p. 65 — n. 36 — *Ibid.,* p. 47, says, "Albert S. Edwards, son of Mr. and Mrs. Ninian W. Edwards, years later said that the cause of the break in the engagement was the opposition and disapproval of his parents."

p. 66 — n. 37 — Basler, ed., *Collected Works,* Vol I, p. 282.

p. 67 — n. 38 — John G. Nicolay, *A Short Life of Abraham Lincoln* (New York, The Century Company, 1903), p. 70, and Thomas, *Abraham Lincoln,* pp. 95-96. Lincoln knew that Logan's exacting methods had contributed to his legal success, but it may have been because Lincoln was receiving only one third of the firm's income that he became restless. However that may be, in December of 1844 he opened an office of his own with young William Herndon as his partner.—*Ibid.*

p. 69 — n. 39 — Tarbell, *Footsteps of Lincolns,* pp. 245-247. *Ibid.,* p. 246, states that Lincoln chose broadswords and certain conditions and distances which made a situation that was ludicrous because Shields' arms and legs were short while Lincoln's were long, giving Lincoln every advantage and no doubt intended by Lincoln to point out to Shields the absurdity of the whole affair.

Friends of Lincoln and Shields, however, saw that the affair could become serious, and they explained to Shields that the letter which irritated him most had been written by another whom Lincoln was protecting. The duel was then called off. Lincoln never again used satire even toward those who used it against him. Instead, he cultivated patience and forgiveness, by which he is lovingly recalled.

p. 70 — n. 40 — Randall, *Mary Lincoln,* p. 64. *Ibid.,* pp. 70-71, tells us that when the Ninian Edwardses learned of Lincoln's and Mary's intentions to marry, they insisted that the wedding be held in their home—and so it was, witnessed only by a few close friends, and with the Reverend Charles H. Dresser officiating.

p. 72 — n. 41 — Ruth Painter Randall, *Lincoln's Sons* (Boston: Little, Brown and Company, 1955), p. 13.
— n. 42 — *Ibid.,* p. 14.

p. 73 — n. 43 — Randall, *Mary Lincoln,* pp. 84-85, points out that Mary worried perhaps unduly over finances, an anxiety which was to plague her throughout life. But there was no cause for alarm now, for Lincoln was actually making a down payment of $750 to the Reverend Charles Dresser for his new story-and-a-half house for which the Lincolns were to pay a total of $1,200 plus a lot which Lincoln already owned in the city.—Pratt, *Finances of Lincoln, p. 63.*

p. 77 — n. 44 — Lincoln's reply to Cartwright's charge was by means of a statement carried in the *Illinois Gazette* of Lacon, August 15, 1846: "That I am not a member of any Christian Church, is true; but I have never denied the truth of the Scriptures . . . I do not think I could myself, be brought to support a man for office, whom I knew to be an open enemy of, and scoffer at, religion."—*See* Basler, ed., *Collected Works,* Vol. I, pp. 382-383, for the full statement of which the above quote is but the most pertinent portion.

p. 78 — n. 45 — Thomas, *Abraham Lincoln,* pp. 116-117. The Lincolns and their two boys had started for Washington, October 25, 1847, by way of Mary Todd Lincoln's childhood home in Lexington, Kentucky.—Pratt, *Chronology,* p. 5.

p. 79 — n. 46 — Polk had been made President in March 1845, and in December had annexed Texas. When the Mexican government had released Texas, they had fixed the southern boundary line on the Nueces river. But the Texans were not satisfied, contending that the boundary was one hundred miles further south at the Rio Grande river. President Polk ordered General Zachariah Taylor to seize the territory between the two rivers. Accordingly, General Taylor moved his army to Fort Brown on the Rio Grande river. The Mexican government asked Taylor to leave the fort, and when he refused, opened fire on April 23, 1846, in protection of Mexican territory.

p. 80 — n. 47 — Ulysses Simpson Grant, *Personal Memoirs of U. S. Grant* (New York, Charles L. Webster & Co., 1885), Vol. I, p. 68.

— n. 48 — Thomas, *Abraham Lincoln,* pp. 126-127.

p. 81 — n. 49 — *Ibid.,* p. 118, states that Lincoln had heard Henry Clay say in a public speech: "This is no war of defence, but one of unnecessary and of offensive aggression. It is Mexico that is defending her firesides, her castles and her altars, not we."

- p. 82 — n. 50 — Randall, *Lincoln's Sons,* p. 21.
- p. 83 — n. 51 — Basler, ed., *Collected Works,* Vol. I, pp. 465-466, 495-496.
- p. 84 — n. 52 — Thomas, *Abraham Lincoln,* p. 115, cites the words here quoted as those which Lincoln used to describe this situation which so distressed him.
- p. 85 — n. 53 — *Ibid.,* p. 117.
- p. 86 — n. 54 — Basler, ed., *Collected Works,* Vol. I, p. 465.
- p. 87 — n. 55 — When Lincoln spoke in Tremont Temple, Boston, he met his cousin, ex-Governor Levi Lincoln, and was invited to his home for dinner. It was later discovered that they were, respectively, sixth and seventh generations removed from Samuel Lincoln, their first ancestor in America. —*See* Waldo Lincoln, *History of the Lincoln Family* (Worcester, Mass., Commonwealth Press, 1923), p. 467.
- p. 89 — n. 56 — Pratt, *Chronology,* p. 5, where we are also told that the one position Lincoln most desired, that of commissioner of the General Land Office, had been assigned to another (Justin Butterfield), and that Lincoln declined appointments as secretary and as governor, respectively, of Oregon Territory.
- p. 93 — n. 57 — Tarbell, *Footsteps of Lincolns,* p. 305.
- p. 97 — n. 58 — Coleman, *Chronology.*
    - n. 59 — Tarbell, *Life of Lincoln,* Vol. II, p. 26; ". . . his father and [step-] mother, who were still living in Coles county . . . were dependent upon him for many of the necessities, as well as all the comforts, of their lives. At intervals ever since he had left home he had helped them; now by saving their land from the foreclosing of a mortgage, now by paying their doctor's bills, now by adding to the cheerfulness of their home . . . visiting them and aiding them in various ways."
- p. 100 — n. 60 — In their bereavement they turned to Dr. James Smith, pastor of the Presbyterian Church, Springfield, for

counsel. The Lincolns attended his church. He proved to be a comfort to them, as was a sermon by William Ellery Channing, given to Lincoln by his good friend, Jesse Fell, of Bloomington. That sermon brought a great change in Lincoln's thinking that established a profound belief in the goodness of God, and in the efficacy of prayer.—Tarbell, *Footsteps of Lincolns,* p. 297.

p. 102 — n. 61 — *Ibid.,* p. 298.

— n. 62 — Harold E. and Ernestine B. Briggs, *Nancy Hanks Lincoln: A Frontier Portrait* (New York, Bookman Associates, 1952), p. 66.

p. 103 — n. 63 — *Ibid.,* p. 64.

p. 104 — n. 64 — Coleman, *Chronology.*

— n. 65 — Beveridge, *Lincoln: 1809-1858,* Vol. I, pp. 584-585. The deep black soil of Illinois made the roads all but impassable, at times, and the construction of the railroads was not only a means of easy and speedy travel, but was also an important way of tying the country together with available markets for all.

p. 105 — n. 66 — Albert Bushnell Hart, *Essentials in American History* (New York, American Book Company, 1905), p. 299.

p. 107 — n. 67 — Henry W. Elson, *Side Lights on American History* (New York, The MacMillan Company, 1900), pp. 300-302, where it is also stated that Douglas had acted upon the counsel of President Franklin Pierce and Secretary of War, Jefferson Davis, the three of them having agreed that the Missouri Compromise should be repealed in order that the advance of slavery might be unhampered.

And Thomas, *Abraham Lincoln,* p. 139, adds the fact that Senator Archibald Dixon of Kentucky had pointed out to Douglas the necessity of explicit repeal of the Missouri Compromise, which Douglas had previously said "no ruthless

Addenda Notes

hand would ever be reckless enough to disturb." In response to Dixon's suggestion, Douglas reluctantly agreed, but correctly predicted "it will raise a hell of a storm."

p. 108 — n. 68 — Douglas, like a gladiator, had fought and won. Bells and cannons broke the stillness of the early hour to hail his victory. But Salmon P. Chase of Ohio is reported to have said to his friend, Charles Sumner of Massachusetts, as they left the Senate in defeat that fateful morning, "They celebrate a present victory, but the echoes they awake will never rest until slavery itself shall die."

Stephen A. Douglas loved his country and intended no harm to the Union, but he had neither properly assessed the North's resentment to his position on the moral issue involved, nor adequately reckoned with the power of Lincoln's doctrine that "right makes might." Yes, bells clanged and cannons boomed in that gray dawn to announce his "victory," but when Douglas returned to Chicago, his home town, he found himself hung in effigy and refused a hearing. *See* Elson, *Side Lights on American History,* pp. 303-309.

p. 110 — n. 69 — Thomas, *Abraham Lincoln,* pp. 164-166. *See* also fuller account by Tarbell, *Footseps of Lincolns,* pp. 328-338. *Cf.* Sandburg, *Prairie and War Years,* pp. 121-123.

p. 111 — n. 70 — Concerning this sacrifice, Lincoln wrote as follows to his friend, William H. Henderson, thereby unconsciously revealing to posterity the real Lincoln: "I could not . . . let the whole political result go to ruin, on a point merely personal to myself."—Basler, ed., *Collected Works,* Vol. II, p. 307.

And Thomas, *Abraham Lincoln,* pp. 146 and 154, shows the full meaning of Lincoln's sacrifice when he reports that while campaigning for Yates, and to bolster Yates' chances, Lincoln, himself, had against his earlier intention become a candidate for the State Legislature. This race he had won, but had resigned to become eligible for the United States Senate race, which he had now lost through his sacrifice for the sake of a cause and a principle.

p. 112 — n. 71 — Carl Sandburg, *Abraham Lincoln: The Prairie Years* (New York: Harcourt, Brace & Company, 1926), Vol. II, pp. 32-34.

p. 114 — n. 72 — Thomas, *Abraham Lincoln,* p. 157. For a fuller and more detailed account, *see* Beveridge, *Lincoln: 1809-1858,* Vol. I, pp. 598-605.

p. 115 — n. 73 — Sandburg, *Prairie Years,* Vol. II, pp. 41-43; Beveridge, *Lincoln: 1809-1858,* Vol. I, pp. 575-583.

p. 118 — n. 74 — Justin H. Forrest, *Lincoln and Historic Illinois* (Springfield, Ill., The Department of Public Works and Buildings, State of Illinois, 1929-1933), p. 40, states that Lincoln said: "If the court please, I would like to introduce this document to show that the moon set at 12:05 a.m. that night, and that the witness could not have seen what he claims he saw—that he could not have distinguished faces or weapons by the light of a moon that was within two hours of setting."

p. 119 — n. 75 — *Ibid.,* p. 41, says: "The court house in which the trial took place has become the Beardstown city hall since the county seat was moved to Virginia, [Illinois] but it is . . . the same building . . ."

p. 121 — n. 76 — Harry E. Pratt, " 'Judge' Abraham Lincoln," *Journal of the Illinois State Historical Society* (Springfield, Ill., Illinois State Historical Library), Spring 1955, pp. 28-39.

p. 122 — n. 77 — Roy P. Basler, ed., *Abraham Lincoln: His Speeches and Writings* (New York, The World Publishing Company, 1946), pp. 372-381.

p. 125 — n. 78 — Thomas, *Abraham Lincoln,* p. 184.

p. 126 — n. 79 — Tarbell, *Footsteps of Lincolns,* pp. 356-357, quotes the following from the New York *Evening Post:* ". . .

Addenda Notes

a perfect rush is made for the grounds; a column of dust is rising to the heavens and fairly deluging those who are hurrying on through it. Then the speakers come, with flags, and banners, and music, surrounded by cheering partisans . . . the signal for shouts that rend the heavens. They are introduced . . . amid prolonged and enthusiastic cheers . . . interrupted by frequent applause, and they sit down finally amid the same uproarious demonstrations . . ."

p. 127 — n. 80 — The North held that all Territories and States were under Federal authority, and that all States through the Federal Constitution were *united into one,* with limited rule to the States; the South held that each State was an independent unit and sovereign in its rights, and that the States were merely leagued together, but not united.

p. 135 — n. 81 — Sandburg, *Prairie and War Years,* pp. 163-165; Thomas, *Abraham Lincoln,* pp. 201-204; and, for the full speech, *see* Basler, ed., *Lincoln: Speeches and Writings,* pp. 517-539.

p. 137 — n. 82 — *Ibid.,* p. 536. In the main body of the speech, Lincoln had said: ". . . of our thirty-nine fathers who framed the original Constitution, twenty-one—a clear majority of the whole—certainly understood that no proper division of local from federal authority, nor any part of the Constitution, forbade the Federal Government to control slavery in the federal territories; while all the rest probably had the same understanding . . . This is all Republicans ask—all Republicans desire—in relation to slavery. As those fathers marked it, so let it be again marked, as an evil not to be extended . . ."—*Ibid.,* pp. 523, 526.

p. 140 — n. 83 — *See* Kyle, *Lincoln in Decatur,* pp. 100-107.

p. 143 — n. 84 — Randall, *Mary Lincoln,* pp. 179 and 186; Thomas, *Abraham Lincoln,* p. 214.

p. 144 — n. 85 — *Ibid.,* pp. 214-215.

p. 147 — n. 86 — *Ibid.,* pp. 222-223.

p. 148 — n. 87 — *Ibid.,* p. 231, reports: "Every day brought its horde of office-seekers; they descended on him in such numbers that Springfield's hotels and boarding-houses were crammed and the overflow put up in sleeping-cars. With every mail came a cascade of letters . . ."

p. 150 — n. 88 — All through the North, rallies, barbecues, torchlight processions by Republican Wide-Awakes in gay uniforms, with bands, glee clubs, floats, banners and speakers moving in rail-fence-like zigzag, deepened the patriotic fervor of all. Five campaign biographies of Abe had been published and widely distributed by June 1860, including one by Dean Howells which Lincoln meticulously corrected.

p. 152 — n. 89 — Years later when James H. Crowder became State Commander of the Illinois Grand Army of the Republic, he had a gavel made from that walnut cane which he had received from Lincoln's own hand. This gavel is now owned and treasured by his grandson, the Reverend Orville Crowder Miller of Urbana, Illinois.

p. 153 — n. 90 — John G. Nicolay, *A Short Life of Abraham Lincoln* (New York, The Century Co., 1903), p. 176, says that "in his annual message to Congress he [Buchanan] announced the fallacious and paradoxical doctrine that though a State had no right to secede, the Federal government had no right to coerce her to remain in the Union. Nor could he [Buchanan] justify his non-action . . ." Lincoln was helpless so long as Buchanan thus remained inactive, and during these months secession grew in power.

p. 154 — n. 91 — J. G. Randall, *Lincoln the President: Springfield to Gettysburg* (New York: Dodd, Mead & Company, 1945), Vol. I, p. 194, reports "the popular vote: Lincoln 1,866,452; Douglas 1,376,957; Breckinridge 849,781; Bell 588,879."

Addenda Notes

p. 161 — n. 92 — Basler, ed., *Lincoln: Speeches and Writings,* pp. 568-570.

p. 162 — n. 93 — Kyle, *Lincoln in Decatur,* p. 121, says: "The train . . . consisted of two passenger cars, a baggage car, and a decorated engine . . ."

p. 163 — n. 94 — *Ibid.,* pp. 121-122, states that among the thirty-six aboard were President-elect Lincoln; his political associates Governor Richard Yates, John Moore, Orville H. Browning, Norman B. Judd, Ebenezer Peck, Ozias M. Hatch, Jesse K. Dubois; Lincoln's son, Robert, and some other young men of Bob's age; officers of the Great Western (Wabash) Railroad, Clint C. Tilton, president, F. W. Bowen, division superintendent, and W. C. Whitney, conductor; Allan Pinkerton of Pinkerton Detective Agency, Chicago; several reporters, including Henry Villard of the *New York Herald;* soldiers; Lincoln's private secretaries, John Nicolay and John Hay; bodyguards Ward H. Lamon and Elmer E. Ellsworth; and brother-in-law and physician, Dr. William S. Wallace. Others boarded enroute.

p. 164 — n. 95 — *Ibid.,* pp. 127-138.

p. 165 — n. 96 — "Henry Villard, *New York Herald* correspondent, filed this dispatch to his newspaper:

'Arrival at Decatur

'Decatur, Feb. 11 — 9:30 A.M.

'An immense multitude awaited the arrival of the train at the depot, and burst out in enthusiastic cheers as it moved up. The President left his car and moved rapidly through the crowd, shaking hands to the right and left. After a stoppage of a few minutes the train proceeded.'"

— n. 97 — *Ibid.,* p. 124.

p. 166 — n. 98 — Thomas, *Abraham Lincoln,* pp. 240-241, reports that word had come as the special train crossed the State of New York to the city of Albany, that Jefferson Davis had been administered the oath of office as President of the Confederacy, and that "an actress, Maggie Mitchell, had danced on the Stars and Stripes."

p. 170 — n. 99 — *Ibid.,* pp. 242-244, states that Lincoln had been warned twice of a plot to assassinate him in Baltimore. The first had come from the detective, Allan Pinkerton, who was employed by S. M. Felton, president of the Philadelphia, Wilmington & Baltimore Railroad. The second had been a note sent from General Winfield Scott and Senator William H. Seward, and carried in person by the latter's son, Frederick, to Lincoln while in Pennsylvania.

Felton and Pinkerton called on Norman B. Judd to discuss the matter. The latter called in Lincoln. It was decided that since the plots were so convincing, Lincoln should not be subjected to undue exposure. Accordingly a counterplot was laid, that Lincoln should take another train from Harrisburg to Washington, to pass through Baltimore before the time scheduled for Lincoln's "Special" and while the plotters slept.

At the Camden Station in Baltimore, accompanied by Ward H. Lamon, his burly bodyguard, Lincoln took a special sleeping car coupled to a through-train to Washington, where they arrived at dawn and Lincoln went immediately to the Willard Hotel. *Cf.* Nicolay, *Short Life of Lincoln,* pp. 172-174.

INDEX

Adams, John Quincy: death, character of, 88.

Albany, Ill.: Abe Lincoln's survey of, 40a, 41.

Allen, Dr. John: of New Salem, 31; treats Abe Lincoln, 50.

Armstrong, Hannah: intercedes for son "Duff," 118.

Armstrong, John (Jack): of Clary's Grove boys, of New Salem, 31; challenges Abe Lincoln to wrestle, is beaten, calls off gang, 28; Black Hawk War, enlists with Abe, 33.

Armstrong, William (Duff): Lincoln pleads with jury at trial of, 14d; Lincoln represents, 114, clears, of murder charge, 118-119.

Ashmun, George: notifies Lincoln of nomination, 14h, 144.

Atchison, Kans.: 134.

Assembly, Legislative: Abe Lincoln, unsuccessful candidate for, 32, 34; Abe Lincoln, member of, 42, 44-45, 51, 51a, 52-53; historic Tenth Session of, plans transportation improvements, moves capital from Vandalia to Springfield, 52-53; defeat recalled, 77.

Baker, Edward Dickinson: 74.

Baltimore, Md.: plot, 169-170.

Bates, Edward: 142.

Beecher, Henry Ward: 135.

Bell, John: 147.

Berry, William F.: of New Salem, 31; Abe Lincoln's partner in store, dies, Lincoln assumes debt, 35, 73.

Bible: Abe Lincoln reads, 91.

Black Hawk: photo of, 14b; War, 32a, 33.

Bloomington, Ill.: Abe Lincoln's "lost speech," 110.

Breckinridge, John C.: 147.

Brown, John: 134.

Bryant, William Cullen: 136.
Buchanan, James: President of U.S., distresses Abe Lincoln by inactivity, 153; character of, 157; hesitates to stop secession, 164; bachelor, receives Lincolns, 172.
Burns, Robert: 38.
Calhoun, John: selects Abe Lincoln as deputy surveyor, 41.
Calhoun, John C.: 107.
Cameron, Rev. John M.: Abe Lincoln casts first known vote, boards in home of, 26; of New Salem, 31.
Cameron, Simon: 142.
Cartwright, Peter: famed evangelist, Abe Lincoln's opponent, won State Assembly seat, 1832; Lincoln, in 1846, refutes false charges of, and wins seat in Congress, 77.
Champaign Co., Ill.: Abe Lincoln in courtroom of, 108.
Charleston, Ill.: Coles Co. court, Abe visits relatives, 97.
Chase, Salmon P.: 142, 146.
Chicago, Ill.: 1860, National Republican Wigwam, 14g; Convention, Lincoln nominated for Presidency, 142-143.
Clary's Grove boys (gang): 31; challenge Abe Lincoln to wrestle, leader Armstrong, beaten, calls off gang, 28; enlist with Abe for Black Hawk War, 33.
Clay, Henry: 105, 107, 113.
Clay-Thomas Compromise: admits Missouri, slave state, 105.
Concord, N.H.: 138.
Congress: Abe Lincoln wins seat, serves in, 77, 79-81; 84-85; 87-90; extension-of-slavery debate in, 123.
Constitution: of the United States, 135; Party, 147.
Cooper Union: 136.
Court: Houses, in Decatur and Sullivan, 14e; Circuit, Lincoln travels the, 14e, 32a, 59-61, 68; cases of, 73, 98, 120, 133; Supreme, 89, 120; Circuit, 89, 91-92; Moultrie, 94; Charleston, 97; relaxation from, 99; cases pending, 102; of Champaign Co., 109; circuit by train, 112; important cases of, 114-116, 118-120; "Judge" Lincoln, 121; Decatur cases, 164.

Index

Crowder, James H. (Jim): at ten, rides horse with father to court, Moultrie Co., meets Abe Lincoln, 96; pledge to Lincoln, 152; 165.

Crowder, Robert (Uncle Bobby): attends court, Moultrie Co., admires Lawyer Abe Lincoln, 94; takes son James to court, talks to Lincoln, introduces Jim, 95-96.

Davis, David: Judge of Sangamon Courts, 1856; photo of, 14c; appoints Abe Lincoln acting judge, 121.

Davis, Jefferson: inaugurated, President of Confederacy, 157.

Debates: instructional, at New Salem, 43; Lincoln-Douglas, 1858, photo of, 14g; show oratorical, political giants; opposite standards, ideas of government and of slavery of, 124-126; results of, 128, 131.

Debt: on Lincoln-Berry store, 35, 73.

Decatur, Ill.: 20, 32a; site of State Republican Convention; receives Abe Lincoln as political leader, names him "Rail-Splitter" candidate for U.S. President, 140-141; throng meets Lincoln's inaugural train, 165.

Democracy: 32, 123, 132.

Democratic Party: 42; urges Polk's expansion of land for slavery, 79; strong for slavery, 80; plans to bar Abe Lincoln from 2nd Congressional term, 81; Douglas and, 107; Lincoln sacrifices to, 111; controls Congress, 123; extravagance of, 145; split three ways, extremists for secession, 147; shows hate of Republican winners, vows revenge, 167.

Doniphan, Kans.: 134.

Douglas, Stephen A.: photo of, 14c; 32a, 68, 113; U. S. Senator from Illinois, orator, desires Presidency, uses Kansas-Nebraska act, 107; manages repeal of Missouri Compromise, 108; opposed by Abe Lincoln, 109, for seat in Senate, 111, 122, 124-128, wins Senate seat but loses popularity to Lincoln, 128, 131, 133; strongest Democratic rival of Lincoln for Presidency, but though he stumps entire campaign, loses election, 147.

Dover, N.H.: 138.

Dresser, Rev. Charles: photo of, 14c; marries Abe Lincoln and Mary Todd, 70; sells house to Abe Lincoln, 73.

Edwards, Matilda: 68.

Edwards, Ninian W.: photo of home of, 14e; 51a, 53, 57, 64.

Effie Afton case: 114.

Faith: 5, 21, 92.

Fell, Jesse W.: 146.

Felton, S. M.: 170.

Fillmore, Millard: 84.

Founding Fathers: 135, 137.

Francis, Mrs. Simeon: reunites Abe Lincoln and Mary Todd, 70.

Frémont, John C.: 117, 121.

Freeport Doctrine: 127.

Globe Tavern: photo of, 14e; first dwelling place of Abe and Mary Lincoln, 71; too noisy, 72.

God: 58, 65, 77, 90, 113, 156, 159, 161, 173.

Godbey, Russell: Abe Lincoln surveys farm of, 41.

Gorin, Jerome K.: 165.

Graham, Mentor: photo of, 14c; suggests to Abe Lincoln a speech remedy, lends him books, 29; of New Salem, 31; aids Abe to learn surveying, 41; hears Abe and Ann Rutledge recite, 47.

Grammar, Kirkham's: Abe Lincoln learns from, 29-30.

Green, Squire Bowling: of New Salem, 31; helps Abe Lincoln with law study, allows Abe to try cases, 37; with Abe at burial of Ann Rutledge, 50.

Hanks, John: makes produce shipping agreement with Offutt; helps Abe Lincoln to Springfield, to build boat, then on to St. Louis, 22; carries "Rail-Splitter" banner at State Republican Convention, Decatur, Ill., 140; meets Lincoln's inaugural train at Decatur stop, 165.

Harrison, William Henry: soldier-President, helps make West great, 113.

Hartford, Conn.: 138.

Hay, Milton: 139.

Herndon, William H.: photo of office of, 14d; Lincoln's 3rd law partner, 116, 179.

Hill, Samuel: of New Salem, 31; postmaster, loses job, 36.

Illinois: 20, 32a, 51a; *see* Assembly, Lincoln (Abe).

Illinois Central Railroad: (I.C.), 102, 104, 112, 114.

Internal Improvements Bill: *see* Assembly, Lincoln (Abe).

Jefferson, Thomas: buys Louisiana Territory, 105.

Johnston, John D.: Abe Lincoln's stepbrother, accompanies him to New Orleans, 22; returns with Abe, 24-25; shirks responsibility of aiding Tom Lincoln, 97.

Johnston, Sarah (Bush): *see* Lincoln, Sarah (Bush).

Judd, Norman B.: 146.

Kansas-Nebraska Act: planned issue for Douglas, 107; threatens power of Missouri Compromise, 108-109, 117.

Kelso, Jack: blacksmith, New Salem, 31; takes Abe Lincoln fishing, quotes classics, 38.

Kirkham's Grammar: 29-30.

Lamon, Ward Hill: one of Abe Lincoln's bodyguards, on inaugural and special trains to Washington, 169-170.

Law: 32a, 35, 40, 42, 47, 54, 55, 59, 67, 73, 98-99; cases, 112, 114-116, 118-121, 164.

Leavenworth, Kans.: 134.

Legislature, Illinois: 32, 44, 47, 49, 51, 51a, 52, 77; *see* Assembly, Lincoln (Abe).

Lexington, Ky.: 62, 82, 86.

Lincoln, Abraham (Abe): photos of, 14a, f; character of the man, 5; map of New Salem, home of, 20; map of Illinois, travels of, 32a; growth of, 21; heads for New Orleans, builds boat, 22; photo of, 14b; shows skill, 23; in New Orleans, sees slave trade, makes resolve; sells cargo and flatboat, takes steamer to St. Louis, reports to Offutt, 24; chosen as storekeeper, 25; begins work in Offutt store, pleases, entertains, reads, 26; makes many friends, becomes "Honest Abe," 27; wrestles, overcomes Jack Armstrong, 28; thirsts for knowledge, reads, 29; acquires perfect English, 30; associates of, 14e, 31; enters politics, 1832, candidate for State Legislature, 32; captain in Black Hawk War, 14f, 33; returns from war; helps farmers, speaks political views, speaks at Springfield, Ill., defeated for election, 34; buys share in Berry store, assumes, eventually pays off, store debt, 35; becomes New Salem postmaster, carries mail in high hat, 14d, 36; reads, practices law, 35-36; tries first case, instructed by Bowling Green, 37; goes fishing with Jack Kelso, learns classics, 38; strives for poise, 39; studies Blackstone, argues imaginative cases, 40; survey map, handwriting and signature of, 40a; studies surveying, becomes deputy surveyor, 41; again candidate, 1834, for State Assembly, wins, decides to make law his profession, 42; joins Men's Debating Club, 43; as legislator, buys clothes, goes to capital, at Vandalia, learns politics and lawmaking, 44-45; comforts Ann Rutledge, helps her hide hurt pride, 46; befriends, entertains Ann, 47; returns from State Assembly, takes walk with Ann; mourns Ann's death, 49; has fever, refuses rest, surveys, nurses sick, 50; legislation and social position of, 51a; recognition in Legislature, 52; with Long Nine, gets capital moved to Springfield, 52-53; moves to Springfield, 54; passes law examination, becomes law partner of John Todd Stuart, 14d, 55; enters Springfield social life, 57; uses wit with logic to win law cases, becomes a leader, 58; Electoral College candidate, 59; enjoys riding court circuit, 14d; social life of county seats, 60; meets Mary Todd, dances with her, 62; goes with Mary Todd, falls in love, 63; courtship chilled, pride hurt, 64; decides, and on Jan. 1, 1841, breaks engagement to Mary, 65; becomes Judge Stephen T. Logan's law partner, gains fame, 67; keeps company with Matilda Edwards, 68; assumes blame for his and Mary Todd's "Rebecca" letters against Shields;

challenged by Shields to duel which is stopped by friends, 69; invited to tea, again meets Mary Todd; marries her, 14e, 70; secures room and board for two at Globe Tavern, 14e, 71; has first son, Robert Todd; moves to three-room house, 72; buys a home, 14e, 73; has second son, Edward (Eddie), 74; candidate for U. S. Congress, 77; elected, takes rooms in Washington, D. C.; entertains with stories, 14f, 78; writes bill to free slaves in District of Columbia, 80; Democrats plan to oust, 81; lonely, worried without family, 82; shops for hose requested by wife, writes questions about his sons, shows anxiety about his family, 83; campaigns, 1848-1849, in East; attends National Convention, sees Whigs nominate Taylor and Fillmore; sees slave depots near capitol, resolves to present his anti-slavery bill, 84; receives good news from Mary about his sons, 86; gains respect, social standing, 87; serves on Congressional committee honoring John Quincy Adams, 88; tries Supreme Court case, returns to Illinois, 89; soon to lose son Eddie and father, 90; back on circuit, gains knowledge, culture, 91-92; character growth of, 93; in Moultrie county court, greets Robert Crowder (Uncle Bobby), tells James Crowder purpose of courts, 96; visits parents, aids father, 97; builds greater law practice, improves speech, 98; enjoys circuit trail, returns home happy, 14d, 99; cares for ailing son, Eddie, 100; grief assuaged by Christmas gift, new-born son, William (Willie), 101; receives news of father's death; grief-stricken, continues urgent court cases, evaluates father, 101-104; calls Thomas, his fourth son, "Tad," tries to help his speech defect, 106; resolves to save Missouri Compromise, 108; campaigns for Yates, shows growth as statesman, 109; casts spell on Bloomington listeners to his "lost speech," 110; seeks Senate seat in 1854; sacrifices race to Trumbull, Free-soiler, 111; makes speaking dates and Circuit Court by train, 112; place of, among the West's great, 113; wins important law cases, 114-115; ridiculed, rebuffed by Edwin M. Stanton, 115-116; frees "Duff" Armstrong from murder charge, 14d, 118-119; reaches heights of law, respect, 120; acts as circuit judge, 121; in 1858, Republican senatorial candidate, 122; debates with Douglas, photo of, 14g, corners him by drawing Freeport Doctrine from him, 124-127; loses election to Douglas, wins in defeat, 128; vows to reach heights, free land from slavery, 131-132; styled orator, 133; speaks in many places, 134-135, 138; greeted as celebrity at Cooper Union, acclaimed, recognized as a national leader, 136-139; at Republican State Convention, 1860, Decatur, Ill., greeted with slogan, "Rail-Splitter"; urged for President, 140-141; nominated for President, 1860, Republican National Convention, Chicago, Ill.; receives official notification, 14h, 142-144; made no campaign speeches, receives news and visitors, expresses views, 146-148; termed press and opposition jibes, "campaigners' brew"; was opposed by four for Presidency, 149-150; watches Springfield campaign demonstration, photo of, 14h; receives loyalty pledge, 152; sits in State House on election day; reviews campaign, Buchanan's inactivity, dividing country; votes, walks home, 153; receives news of election as President, 154; realizes secession is real, 155; lets house, sells furnishings, forms inaugural address, chooses Cabinet; visits stepmother, Sarah Bush Lincoln, 156; feels chagrin at secession of six states, 157; takes last walk on prairie fields, feels no need, but yields to plan for armed guards on trip to Washington, 158; morning prayer of, 159; boards train to leave Springfield, walks to rear to speak, 160; bids friends farewell, commends all to God, 161; as train nears Decatur (photo of, 14h), recalls past there, 164; met by throng of friends, 165-166; speaks to many on twelve-day trip to Washington, 168; rushes by special sleeping car ahead of schedule, 169-171; in Washington, receives callers; accompanied by Mary, pays respects to President Buchanan, 172; asks for simple inaugural parade, chief respect to be paid to nation's flag, 173; spends restless night, March 3, 1861, reviewing past, and plans to save nation, 174.

Lincoln, Edward (Eddie): birth of, 2nd son of Abe and Mary, 74; taken by Mary to visit grandfather, 78, 83; Mary's letter about, 86; illness, death of, 100-101; tombstone of, 14e.

Lincoln, Levi: 87.

Lincoln, Mary (Todd): for early life, *see* Todd, Mary; as bride of Abe, lives at Globe Tavern, 14e, 71; bears son, Robert, desires more room and quiet, moves to Fourth Street, 72; worries about cost of new Eighth Street home, 73; bears 2nd son, Edward (Eddie), 74; with two sons, accompanies Abe to Washington, D.C.; four months later, leaves for Lexington, Ky., with sons, 14f, 78; guest in father's home, writes love letters to Abe, 82; writes Abe for son's plaid hose, 83; writes Abe of their sons, 86; with Abe in Springfield, cares for dying "Eddie," 100; bears 3rd son, William (Willie), 101; bears 4th son, Thomas (Tad), 106; hears Abe's report of his Presidential nomination and election, 143, 154; for safety, follows with sons on regular train; rebels, joins Presidential train, 167; accompanies Abe to call on President Buchanan, 172.

Lincoln, Robert Todd: first child of Abe and Mary, is named for grandfather, 72; Abe dreams about, 83; news of, 86; on inaugural train, 163.

Lincoln, Sarah (Bush): Abe's stepmother, photo of, 14c; visited by Abe, shows pride and alarm, 156.

Lincoln, Thomas (Tom): Abe's father, weakened by malaria, is dismayed by shirking stepson, John Johnston; Abe aids, 97; death, burial, character of, 102-104.

Lincoln, Thomas (Tad): photo of, 14f; birth of, named for Abe's father; speech defect of, 106; goes with father on walk, 158.

Lincoln, William Wallace (Willie): 3rd son of Abe and Mary, photo of, 14f; birth of, 101; goes with father on walk, 158.

Logan, Judge Stephen T.: photo of, 14c; becomes Abe Lincoln's 2nd law partner, 67; political support of, 146.

Long Nine, The: votes to move capital to Springfield, 53.

Malaria: causes Ann Rutledge's death, 49; invades most homes, 50; leaves Tom Lincoln weak, 97.

Matteson, Joel A.: 111.

McLean, Justice John: 142.

McNeil (McNamar), John: takes Ann Rutledge everywhere, disappears, 46; ceases to write to Ann, 47.

Medill, Joseph: 146.

Metsker, James Preston: death of, "Duff" Armstrong accused of murder of, 118-119.

Mexican War: 79-81.

Millikin, James: 165.

Missouri: part of Louisiana Territory, Compromise makes it slave state, 105; Compromise threatened, 108; Compromise repealed, 111; Compromise supported by Republicans, 117.

New Orleans, La. (Ol' Orleans): appearance, people, slave market, Abe's impressions of, 24-25; 32a.

New Salem, Ill.: maps of, 20, 32a; meets Abe Lincoln, dam episode, 23; welcomes Abe Lincoln, 25, 27; folks of, 31; social life of, 39-40; Debating Club of, 43.

New York: Cooper Union of, 136, 138; State of, 166.

Norwich, Conn.: 138.

Offutt, Denton (Dent); gets Abe Lincoln to steer produce boat to Ol' Orleans, 22; receives report from Abe, is pleased, 24; plans for Abe to manage New Salem store, 25; opens store, 1831, Abe in charge, 26-27; praises Abe's brawn, wrestling, 28; of New Salem, 31.

Oglesby, Richard (Dick): plans 1860 State Republican Convention "Rail-Splitter" banner, Decatur, Ill., 140; meets Abe Lincoln's inaugural train at Decatur, 165.

Palmer, Judge John M.: offers resolution at State Republican Convention in Decatur, Ill., proposing Abe Lincoln's nomination for President, 141.

Pinkerton, Allan: detective, rides inaugural train, 170.
Politics: 32, 32a, 34, 42, 44-45, 51-53, 54-59, 67, 79-90, 105-111, 117, 121-128, 131, 134-154.
Polk, President James K.: by Mexican War, seizes land for slavery extension, 79; victorious in Mexican War, shamed nation with false claim, 81.
Prayer: 5, 65, 90, 156, 159.
Republican Party: organized, nominates John C. Frémont for President, 117; at Springfield, Ill., 1858, nominates Abe Lincoln for U. S. Senate, hears "House Divided" speech, 122; Decatur Convention of, 140-141; Chicago Convention of, 14g, 142-143; platform, supporters of, 145-146; 167.
Rutledge, Ann: of New Salem, 31; pretty daughter of tavern keeper; goes with McNeil, perhaps engaged, pride hurt by his unexplained disappearance, 46; goes everywhere with Abe Lincoln, tells Abe he will be renowned, 47; father's financial reverses cause move to farm, 48; walks with Abe, hears of State Assembly; sickens, dies, 49; burial of, 50.
Saint Louis (Saint Lou): Abe reports to Offutt from, of his trip to New Orleans, 24; Offutt stocks new store from, 25.
Sangamon: river on which Abe Lincoln canoed to Springfield, 22, 32a; county, Judge of, 121.
Schurz, Carl: 146.
Secession: six states planning, 153; South Carolina begins, other states talking of, 155; six states of, confederated, 157; haters, plotters against Lincoln's life evaded, 169.
Seward, William H.: recognized leader of Republican Party, 87; Abe Lincoln's strongest competitor for Presidency, 142-143; campaigns for Lincoln, 145; Thurlow Weed's man, 149.
Shakespeare, William: 38, 63, 91.
Shields, James: state auditor, 1842; challenges Abe Lincoln to duel over "Rebecca" letters, 69.
Shipley, Reason: Abe Lincoln surveys farm of, 41.

Short, James: of New Salem, 31.

Slavery: Abe Lincoln sees New Orleans market of, 24; extended by James K. Polk, Mexican War, 79-81; Abe Lincoln drafts bill to free District of Columbia of, 80; redrafts same, 84; Missouri Compromise limited, 105; Abe Lincoln opposes, 121-122, 127, 131-132, 135, 137; opposed by 1860 Republican platform, 145; six Southern States favor, prepare to fight for, 157.

Smoot, Squire Coleman: of New Salem, 31.

Speech, by Abe Lincoln: site of first political, 20; campaign, in Springfield, 34; in Congress, Spot Resolution, 79; at Bloomington, "Lost," 110; "House Divided," 122; in Lincoln-Douglas debates, 124-128, 131; Cooper Union, 135-137; Farewell, 161.

Speed, Joshua Fry (Josh): photo of, 14c; lets Abe Lincoln share lodgings above his furniture store in Springfield, Ill., 54.

Sprigg, Mrs. Ann G.: Lincolns live at Washington, D. C. boardinghouse of, 14f, 78.

Springfield, Ill.: Abe Lincoln's canoe trip to, 22, 32a; in 1832, Abe speaks at, 34; in 1837, Abe moves to, 54; sprawling prairie town; as capital, highlights, social life of, 32a, 51a, 53-57, 62-63; Republican State Convention at, nominates Abe Lincoln for U. S. Senate, hears Lincoln's "House Divided" speech, 122; awaits 1860 Presidential election results, hears Abe Lincoln wins, celebrates, 142-143; rally, huge parade, for Abe Lincoln, 151-152; on Election Day, 153-155; Abe Lincoln's awareness of task, 159; farewell of, 14h, 160-162.

Stanton, Edwin M.: Eastern lawyer, derides, rebuffs Abe Lincoln, 115-116.

Stephens, Alexander H.: 87.

Stuart, Major John T.: photo of, 14c; Abe Lincoln's social friend, first law partner, 54-55, 67.

Sullivan, Ill.: Moultrie county seat, 14d, 94; "Uncle Bobby" and son James Crowder meet Abe Lincoln at court in, 96.

Swett, Leonard: 146.

Taylor, Zachary: 84, 87.

Todd, Mary: photo of, 14c; meets, dances with Abe Lincoln, 62; lets Abe go with her, reads with, falls in love with him, 63-64; released from engagement by Abe Lincoln, 65; wooed by Webb and Stephen Douglas, 68; writes "Rebecca" letter satirical of Shields, 69; learns Abe Lincoln risked duel to shield her; meets Abe at Mrs. Francis' Tea, becomes Mrs. Abraham Lincoln, 14e, 70; *see* Lincoln, Mary (Todd).

Tombs, Robert: 87.

Transportation: circuit lawyer Lincoln on horseback, 14d; roads flooded, Abe Lincoln and John Hanks go to Springfield by canoe, build flatboat for trip to New Orleans, 22, 32a; at New Salem dam, 23; return by steamer, to Saint Louis, 24; fishing skiff, 38; stage from New Salem to Vandalia, 44; bill to extend railroads, good country roads, 52; railroads bind East to West, trains have sleeping cars, 112; I. C. and *Effie Afton* law case, rivalry of rail and river, 114; of Lincoln *vs.* Douglas, 125; of populace to Lincoln-Douglas debates, 126; Abe Lincoln's inaugural train, make-up and passengers, 160-163; sleeping car, with President-elect Abe Lincoln, *switched* from inaugural "Special" to regular through train, to avoid Baltimore plotters, 170.

Troy, Kans.: 134.

Trumbull, Lyman: 111.

Ullrich, John: 165.

Wallace, Dr. William S.: Mary Lincoln's brother-in-law, her 3rd son named for; Abe's personal physician, on inaugural train, 101, 163.

War: Black Hawk, 32a, 33; Mexican, 79-81.

Washington, D. C.: New Salem's request to, 36; Congressman Abe Lincoln in, 78-90; reception of Lincoln "Special," 171.

Washington, George: Abe Lincoln reads life of, 32; Abe compares his task to that of, 161.

Webster, Daniel: 87, 107.
Weed, Thurlow: 149.
Whig Party: 42, 51, 59; supports Abe for Congress, 77, 79; nominates Taylor and Fillmore, 84; sacrifice, 111; joins in organization of Republican Party, 117.
Wilmot, David: patient, authors "Proviso" against slavery extension, 80.
Yates, Richard: 109.